# Coal People

## Life in Southern Colorado's

## Company Towns,

## 1890–1930

by Rick J. Clyne

*Colorado History*
Number 3
1999

ISSN 1091-7438

COLORADO HISTORICAL SOCIETY

**Research and Publications Office**
David Fridtjof Halaas and David N. Wetzel, *directors*

**Publications Director**
David N. Wetzel

***Colorado History* Series Editor**
Steven G. Grinstead

**Book Review Editor**
David Fridtjof Halaas

**Editorial Assistance**
William Philpott, Consultant and Copy Editor

The Colorado Historical Society publishes *Colorado History* to provide a flexible scholarly forum for well-written, documented manuscripts on the history of Colorado and the Rocky Mountain West. Its twofold structure is designed to accommodate article-length manuscripts in the traditional journal style and longer, book-length works which appear as monographs within the series. Monographs and special thematic issues are individually indexed; other volumes are indexed every five years. The Colorado Historical Society disclaims responsibility for statements of fact or opinion made by contributors.

Postage paid at Denver, Colorado

# Contents

# FIGURES

*To Laurie, Bobbie, and Richie*

## ABOUT THE AUTHOR

Rick Clyne is freelance technical writer. Born and raised on Long Island, Clyne has called the West home since 1982, when he transferred to the New Mexico Institute of Mining and Technology as an undergraduate. He received a master's degree in history from the University of Colorado at Denver in 1995. He and his wife, Laurie, live in Denver.

# Preface

While living in New Mexico in the late 1980s, I regularly drove the 450-mile stretch of Interstate 25 between Albuquerque and Denver. I had a small Toyota pickup, which was a little cramped, but the stiff neck was an insignificant price to pay for a weekend of skiing with old college friends. I was in my mid-twenties at the time and working my first real job as a technical writer. Those Friday afternoon winter road trips were pure liberation. I felt as if the road were paved just for me, and my little truck would hum easily over the hills north of Santa Fe and up along Colorado's Front Range.

The road is a friendly one—especially the 250 miles, give or take, between Santa Fe and Pueblo. To the west, the Pecos and Sangre de Cristo mountains accompanied me most of the way. Long before I developed an urge to formally study history, I felt that these mountains had a way of confronting you with the past. I could glance westward at the jagged afternoon sky and sense the ancient Anasazi, or the pueblo dwellers, or the Spanish colonists and their isolated descendants.

Along this stretch, I-25 is like a seam that joins the Rocky Mountains to the plains, extending endlessly to the east. Here reside communities characteristic of the isolated West, towns like Wagon Mound, Springer, and Raton. For fifty or sixty miles, road signs anticipate these places. In a flash I would streak past their lone exits, not needing gas and not hungry enough to lose time.

Raton Pass on the border between New Mexico and Colorado is the midpoint between Albuquerque and Denver. At 7,800 feet, the pass is modest by Rocky Mountain standards, but it offers relief from the previous two hours of straight, flat interstate. On the descent into Colorado I always noticed the ruins of the mission-style church on a hilltop off to the west. There was an exit here called "Morley" that seemed to serve no other purpose than to dare me to pull off and explore the abandoned church. I promised myself I would do just that on the next trip, but I never did.

Right at the bottom of Raton Pass lies the town of Trinidad, Colorado. I'd make a point of slowing down, figuring Trinidad policemen liked ticketing out-of-state drivers oblivious to the momentum gained coming down the pass. Trinidad was slightly larger than the other towns on the route—maybe three exits. The downtown area sits right below the I-25 viaduct, and the buildings have that pragmatic, turn-of-the-century architecture that again beckoned me to stop and check them out. Nope, maybe next time.

North of Trinidad, the Spanish Peaks command the skyline for about thirty miles. Somehow separated long ago from the Sangre de Cristo range standing quietly behind them, these twin, isolated thirteen- to fourteen-thousand-foot mountains are . . . well . . . magnificent. These peaks grew larger as I headed out of Trinidad toward Walsenburg. About ten miles north of town I would pass the desolate exit for Ludlow.

An unknowing traveler might quickly glance around looking for the town of Ludlow, or a truck stop, or anything that would indicate population, and, seeing nothing, shrug and keep going. But I had heard of Ludlow, maybe from a PBS documentary, and I knew vaguely about what had happened there. My road atlas showed a little dot labeled "Ludlow Monument" a quarter-inch or so west of the exit. So one clear, chilly February day—against my urge to make good time into Denver—I decided to get off I 25 and take a look.

The Ludlow Monument is only a couple miles west of the highway. The pavement quickly ends, and the road resembles thousands of other dry gravel tracks that cross the rangeland of the West. Set off alone against the backdrop of southern Colorado's low foothills, the monument site is easily discernable at a distance. Erected by the United Mine Workers of America some years after the massacre, the monument is a proletarian affair. A rectangular, free-standing, white-stone column about twenty feet tall sits atop a three-step platform. Three life-size figures reside at the base of the column. A man, noble and prosaic, stands without emotion, his gaze fixed to the southwest. To his left, a woman sits uncomfortably on the base of the column, exhausted, looking as if she needed a moment to rest. Her head is propped on her bent left arm. She loosely cradles a small child in her right.

The monument marks the site where, in the fall of 1913, striking coal miners and their families—about a thousand people in all—set up a large tent colony after being evicted from their company-owned housing. The strike began in September and dragged on through the following spring. Like so many other Progressive-Era labor conflicts, the strike was violent, replete with sporadic beatings and executions administered by agents on both sides of the picket line. The conflict culminated here, at the tent colony set up adjacent to the Ludlow train depot, with a protracted gun battle between the cold, weary miners and the tense militiamen, who were effectively under the command of the region's coal companies. In the day-long melee, the tent colony burned, and twenty of its inhabitants, including two women and eleven children, died from either gunshots or fire. A bronze plaque mounted to the monument lists their names and ages.

I can't say that I experienced an epiphany standing at the monument dedicated to miners and their kin killed at Ludlow. Although it would be romantic to claim that my decision to pull off the road that winter day inspired me to formally study history and research southern Colorado's coal-mining families, that's just not the case. For me, any inkling of going back to school was still years away.

That's not to say the moment wasn't poignant. Standing alone at that spot and reading the names of the dead did something to me that no book or TV documentary could do. It connected real people—mothers and fathers and children—to the mythlike events that fill the pages of our history books. Frank Rubino, age 23; Lucy Costa, age 4; Frank Petrucci, age 6 months; Patria Valdez, age 37. These were plain people, like me, like my parents, who never expected to lose their lives on the desolate plains of southern Colorado. They weren't generals, queens, diplomats, or the heirs to European thrones. What did they aspire to in life? A warm shelter? A modest income capable of supporting a family? A few drinks with friends on Saturday night?

After my side trip to Ludlow, reading history, which at that time was no more than a hobby for me, became a bit more personal. A subtle yet important shift had occurred in the way I perceived the past. The mythic events of history, whether a British infantry charge on the Somme in 1916 or Rosa Parks's refusal to relinquish her seat on a Memphis bus, became the story of real people. Ludlow was no longer just another violent showdown between labor and management. It was Louis Tikas, age 30; it was Rodgerlo Pedregone, age 6; it was Ferelina Costa, age 27.

And so I hope that a sense of the real people behind the history comes across in the pages of this book. Ironically, if eight decades of coal mining in the region around Trinidad and Walsenburg are remembered at all, they are remembered for the massacre at Ludlow. And that's understandable, given the inherent drama of bloodshed. But to fixate on this one tragic event oversimplifies...

It neglects the complexities of southern Colorado's industrial era. Industrial-scale coal production began in southern Colorado in the 1880s and reached its peak in the late 1910s, during World War I. Production declined steadily thereafter, except for a brief boom during World War II, and the last of the dedicated coal-mining towns shut down in the 1960s. Ludlow is but a brief, albeit horrifying, moment in this eighty-year-long story. For that matter, even the wider struggle to unionize is a relatively minor chapter in a tale that is much more complicated overall.

Tens of thousands of people—including many newly arrived immigrants—lived in the coal-company towns of southern Colorado. Many knew America only through their experiences in these isolated camps. What was it like to be a child in such a town? What did a typical day hold for the wife of a coal miner? What, if any, leisure activities were available to miners and their families? How did a sense of community develop in these industry-dominated camps? What role did the coal companies play in the daily lives of camp residents? These are a few of the broad questions I address in this book. The answers reveal a small slice of America during its transformation into a modern, industrial society, and they indicate that social, cultural, and economic dynamics in the coal towns were more complicated than many popular histories might have us believe.

The history of southern Colorado's coal-mining towns cuts across a number of historiographical subdisciplines. Cultural, social, and economic historians, along with historians of labor, immigration, gender, and business, can all find fertile ground in the camps. Relying heavily on two oral-history collections—the University of Colorado's Coal Project and the Huerfano County Ethno-History Project—I've tried to discover how people lived together, and what their lives were like, on southern Colorado's industrial frontier.

Although this study covers fifty years and hundreds of square miles of the southern Colorado landscape, it points to a number of general conclusions. For one, the act of mining coal dominated all aspects of camp life. Mining was physically demanding, frequently debilitating, and often deadly. Coal miners struggled against the earth, extracting a livelihood from cold, dark rock deep below the surface. They and their families lived knowing that tragedy could strike on any day the mine operated. Death and suffering came without warning—in an unstable slab of slate, a noxious pocket of gas, or an explosive concentration of dust. A subtle tension pervaded the present in the coal towns, and uncertainty colored the future.

But life was not completely bleak. In fact, the communities served as ready-made support systems for a transient mining population. Mining families were highly mobile, moving from camp to camp in search of steady work or better wages. But no matter how recently a family had arrived in a community, the danger and stress of mining coal gave that family an instant sense of commonality, a strong and unique bond with the other camp residents. Even more, a newly arrived family could quickly find an additional sense of belonging in one of the town's ethnic enclaves. Many of the region's coal miners between 1890 and 1933 had immigrated from southern or eastern Europe. Shared danger and the common immigrant experience created an atmosphere of acceptance and tolerance in the coalfield camps.

Finally, in the midst of these occupational and social dynamics, organized labor—the focus of so much historical writing—was a relatively minor influence on the lives of southern Colorado's coal-town families. To be sure, the region was rocked by strikes about once every ten years, as unions battled for solidarity, union recognition, and better living and working conditions. And the unions, primarily the United Mine Workers of America, wielded a considerable amount of power over their members during periods of strike activity. But these periods were relatively short and infrequent. In the wake of each turbulent conflict, the union virtually disappeared, and camp residents carried on their struggles with the mine operators in isolation and on their own.

The pages that follow shed light on these themes and on the lives of the real people who lived, worked, and often died in these company towns. With the help of some remarkably vivid oral histories, I have attempted to reconstruct the lives of miners and their families, and to re-create the communities. As you listen to the voices of coal-camp residents, you will begin to sense the ever-present danger that stalked the miners and settled over the camps like an invisible fog. I hope you will also feel the anticipation and excitement that camp residents felt as they prepared for a Saturday night on the town. Perhaps you will even smell the distinctive ethnic foods that cooked in camp kitchens, filled the workers' lunch boxes, and graced their families' dinner tables. And I suspect you will come to understand the bone-numbing exhaustion that men, women, and even children felt as they collapsed into bed each night, ending yet another day of toil, another day spent scraping out an existence on America's industrial frontier.

# Acknowledgments

This book began as my master's thesis at the University of Colorado at Denver. The UCD history faculty bears full responsibility for making graduate school such an adventure. Mark Foster, my advisor, said on my first day that the work he assigned might seem excessive, but that his goal was to "stretch" us intellectually—to expose us to varying historiographical viewpoints, to force us to think critically, to be prepared to support the arguments we make. I definitely got stretched. I hope Mark sees in these pages a reflection of his work ethic, professionalism, and excellence as an educator.

It was Jim Whiteside who suggested that I look into coal town life; he had seen the need for such work during his doctoral research into coal mine safety regulations in the West. This work is very much a result of Jim's direction, suggestions, critiques, and guidance, and I can say without equivocation that this work would be so much less if I had not had the good fortune to work closely with him.

Mary Conroy and Dick Allen, two Europeanists in the UCD History Department, did not participate directly in my thesis work, but their dedication to teaching and their infectious love for the study of history had a tremendous effect on me.

I would not have completed this work without help from the folks who work at the Colorado Historical Society, the Denver Public Library Western History Department, and the Archives at the University of Colorado at Boulder. Anyone who's dabbled in Colorado history is aware of the in-depth and invaluable assistance available at these research libraries.

I owe a great debt to the people responsible for the two oral history projects on which this work is anchored. With the Colorado Coal Project, completed in 1970s, sociologist Eric Margolis created a priceless record of first-hand accounts about the coal-mining experience. The legacy of this work—the transcripts and videotapes of hundreds of interviews with those who worked the mines and lived in the camps—is available in the Archives at the University of Colorado at Boulder.

Likewise, the Huerfano County Ethno-History project, conducted in the early 1970s by Elaine Baker, contains transcribed interviews with the one-time coal-town residents of Huerfano and Las Animas counties. These materials are maintained in the Huerfano County Library in Walsenburg, Colorado.

The publications staff at the Colorado Historical Society deserves a special nod for turning my academically geared thesis into a book that can be read and—hopefully—enjoyed by a general audience. This is an often overlooked and underappreciated craft, and Dave Wetzel, Steve Grinstead, and especially Bill Philpott, my editor, did a great job engineering the transformation. I hope they are as happy with the result of their efforts as I am.

Finally, this book would never have happened without the people to whom I've dedicated it—my wife Laurie and my parents Bobbie and Richie. There's no substitute in life for the support and sanctuary provided by loved ones.

# Coal People

## Chapter One
# Coalfields, Companies, and Unions

*Unlike manufacturing industries the mining industry can not
choose its location with any reference to labor supply. It must
bring its labor wherever the coal seams run, and they run with
no regard to the adaptability of a region to community or
family life.*
—U.S. WOMEN'S BUREAU, 1925[1]

Iron and coal are the two primary ingredients of industrialization. Iron
ore can be smelted and refined into a variety of products, such as pig iron,
wrought iron, and steel, each of which has different qualities of strength
and malleability. Many of the materials modern society depends upon—
the steel piers and girders used to frame skyscrapers, the reinforcement bar
used to strengthen concrete structures, the various grades of steel used to
build heavy machinery—are derived from iron.

Coal is an excellent industrial-scale fuel. Prior to the nineteenth century, wood was humankind's main source of thermal energy. But wood
could not efficiently generate the tremendous amount of heat needed to fire
smelters, blast furnaces, and other large facilities—the sort of facilities that
increasingly dominated nineteenth-century industry. Coal could. A relatively modest pile of coal could supply the same thermal energy as a giant
stack of wood. Because of its higher energy density, coal could be more
economically transported over greater distances for use in smelters and the
like. It is no coincidence that during the late eighteenth and nineteenth
centuries, nations like Germany, Britain, and the United States—those nations that had access to large stores of iron and coal—were the ones that
industrialized rapidly and evolved into global powers. The availability of
iron and coal contributed mightily to these nations' political and economic
ascent.

Throughout the nineteenth century, America's industrial engine slowly
gained speed. In the early 1800s, Americans burned coal in small amounts—
usually as a domestic fuel, and only in areas where coal seams protruded
through the earth's surface so that the coal could be gathered easily. But as
the pace of industrialization quickened, America's appetite for coal grew

more ravenous. In the three decades from 1800 to 1832, America's annual coal production increased tenfold, from about 100,000 tons to one million tons. But even that was just the beginning. Production increased over one hundredfold in the next half century. By 1885 the United States mined 110 million tons of coal each year. By 1900 the figure had more than doubled to 243 million tons a year, surpassing Britain's output and making the United States the world's largest producer of coal.[2]

The majority of America's industrial-age coal came from the Appalachian states of Pennsylvania, West Virginia, Kentucky, Tennessee, and Virginia, which together combined to produce about four-fifths of the nation's total.[3] Much of the remaining fifth came from the midwestern states of Ohio and Illinois. A small amount came from the western United States— from Colorado, New Mexico, Utah, and Montana, with Colorado being the region's leading producer. But the coalfields of the West were more important than their small output indicates. They allowed heavy industry to develop in the region, which in turn reduced the need to transport finished iron products from the East.

Most of Colorado's coal lies in two great fields: the northern field, which runs along the Front Range in Boulder and Weld counties, and the southern field, which underlies large areas of Las Animas and Huerfano counties. At the turn of the century, minor fields existed elsewhere in the state—most notably in Fremont, Routt, and Gunnison counties—but production in those areas was minimal compared to production in the northern and southern fields.

The bituminous coal produced in Colorado's southern field was particularly well suited to industrial uses.[4] Bituminous coal can be used directly as a source of fuel, for instance in locomotives or homes, or it can be purified into coke, which involves baking the coal slowly, without igniting it, to remove organic matter. Coke burns cleaner and hotter than regular coal. It is the fuel of choice for firing the large blast furnaces that produce steel because burning coke introduces fewer impurities into the molten metal.

The bituminous coal beds of southern Colorado assume the shape of a large backward L (Fig. 1). Beginning about ten miles north of Walsenburg in Huerfano County, the beds run south for fifty miles, paralleling what is now Interstate 25. Near the bottom of Raton Pass, just south of Trinidad in Las Animas County, the seam turns 90 degrees to the west, heading straight up the Purgatoire River valley. About thirty miles of valley stretch between Trinidad and Tercio, the westernmost coal mine on the Purgatoire.

Though small company towns were sprinkled throughout the area,

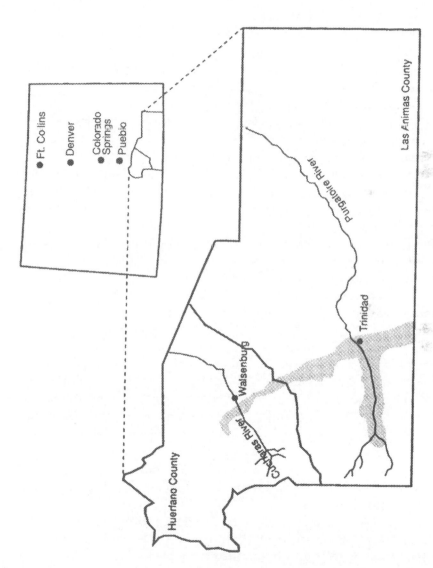

Figure 1. Las Animas and Huerfano Counties

Trinidad and Walsenburg were the two main population centers anchoring the southern Colorado coal-mining industry. Both cities began as traditional plaza communities, founded in the 1850s by Hispanos who had migrated from northern New Mexico. Herding and agriculture allowed these communities to take hold and attain modest self-sufficiency. Although the region's climate is semiarid, the towering peaks of the Sangre de Cristo Range to the west capture enough moisture throughout the year to supply Trinidad and Walsenburg with fresh water. The Purgatoire River begins near the summit of Culebra Peak, flows through Trinidad, and meanders into eastern Las Animas County. The Cucharas River, whose headwaters spring from the awe-inspiring Spanish Peaks, runs through Walsenburg and then turns northeast before emptying into the larger Huerfano River. All of the rivers and streams in Las Animas and Huerfano counties ultimately drain into the Arkansas River on the plains of southeastern Colorado.

The isolated pastoral existence of La Plaza de los Leones—Walsenburg's Hispanic precursor—and of the plaza village at Trinidad lasted only a few short decades. Then, the end of the Civil War brought Colorado a great influx of settlers from the eastern states. Throughout the 1860s and 1870s, Colorado grew toward statehood. Private parties snapped up more and more of the land, and entrepreneurs built more and more of the industrial infrastructure that would be needed to tap the territory's wealth of natural resources.

No part of this infrastructure was more important or more influential than the railroad. Indeed, heavy industry literally arrived in southern Colorado on the rails of General William Palmer's Denver & Rio Grande (D&RG) Railroad. The golden age of coal mining in Colorado also began with these rails. When General Palmer assumed control of the fledgling D&RG in 1873, the company had already begun mining coal in Fremont County under one of its subsidiaries, the Central Colorado Improvement Company. The Cañon mine in Fremont County produced a respectable 13,000 tons of coal in 1873, with about a third of it going to fuel Palmer's narrow-gauge locomotives.[5]

Palmer's vision was an ambitious one: he hoped to expand the D&RG southward to tap the markets of Central America. But the nationwide economic crash of 1873 greatly curtailed these plans. The railroad from Denver had just reached Pueblo when the depression hit, and it would take another three years for the line's main branch to creep into southern Colorado's coalfields. In 1876, the tracks reached El Moro, a D&RG company town five miles north of Trinidad, finally opening the door to large-scale exploitation of the area's vast coal deposits. During the next three years, prosperity returned to America—and to the D&RG. The railroad extended its reach westward, toward the gold and silver boomtowns of the Colorado Rockies, and the company's property holdings grew considerably.

It was common practice in this heyday of industrialization for a rapidly expanding firm to set up a variety of subsidiaries—some of them "real" companies, others only "paper"—in order to defray the costs of conducting business. The ambitious D&RG followed this same strategy, and in fact it was a D&RG subsidiary that would come to dominate the iron and coal industry of southern Colorado. General Palmer, seeking ways to minimize expenses and maximize profits, realized that the railroad could save money by producing its own steel rails. So he consolidated D&RG's subsidiaries in 1879 and built a steel mill in Pueblo—and thus was born the Colorado Coal and Iron Company (CC&I). From its inception, the new company's holdings were substantial, including 13,571 acres of coal land in Huerfano, Las Animas, and Fremont counties and 83,944 acres of agricultural lands along the Arkansas, Cucharas, and Purgatoire rivers. With its landholdings, coal mines, and the new Pueblo steel mill, known as the Bessemer Works, CC&I instantly became the preeminent economic force in the southern part of the state. In 1880, the firm already accounted for half of the coal mined in Colorado.[6]

Still, CC&I enjoyed only marginal success through the 1880s. Building and operating the steel mill in Pueblo was highly capital-intensive, and demand for the mill's steel rails fluctuated. The company had a difficult time operating in the black throughout the decade, turning a profit only on the strength of its real-estate and fuel departments. The real-estate department managed all of the land rented or leased by CC&I, including all of the buildings and dwellings in the coal camps and in Pueblo. When steel production took an upswing in 1890, about 800 men were employed in CC&I's mines, coke ovens, and quarries, and an equal number were employed at the Pueblo steel mill.[7]

In 1892, CC&I merged with Colorado's other large coal interest, the Colorado Fuel Company (CFC), controlled by John C. Osgood. Osgood had come to Colorado from Iowa in 1882 to evaluate coal deposits for the Chicago, Burlington, and Quincy Railroad. Liking what he saw, he and his "Iowa Group" of friends founded the Colorado Fuel Company in 1884. The new firm acted as a coal clearing-house, buying coal from Colorado mines and reselling it to midwestern railroads. Besides CFC, Osgood founded a number of smaller coal-based companies in Colorado between 1884 and 1888. Then he reorganized CFC to consolidate all of his holdings. By the decade's end, half of CFC's 5,500 acres of coal land lay in Las Animas County, and the company's Sopris mine a few miles west of Trinidad was the state's largest single producer.[8]

The merger of Palmer's Colorado Coal and Iron with Osgood's Colorado Fuel Company went smoothly, because both organizations realized it was in their best interests to put an end to their cutthroat competition. Osgood got the best of the deal, thanks to his savvy negotiating skills and CFC's record of success. Stockholders approved the merger in the fall of 1892, and the Colorado Fuel and Iron Company (CF&I) was born. CF&I would reign as the dominant power in Colorado's coal and steel industries for the next sixty years.[9]

John Osgood assumed control of CF&I from its inception, and the firm's vast holdings made it an immediate economic and political force. The new company owned 70,000 acres of coal lands in the state, about half of it located in the southern field. In Las Animas County, CF&I owned the Engleville, Sopris, and Berwind mines; in Huerfano County it held the Walsen, Robinson, Rouse, and Pictou mines. It operated additional mines in Gunnison, Fremont, Garfield, and Pitkin counties. Combined, CF&I's properties contained an estimated 400 million tons of coal.[10]

CF&I weathered the economic crash of 1893 and maintained profitable operations for the rest of the decade. In 1899, the company launched an ambitious four-year improvement plan that would greatly expand the steel mill in Pueblo and bring additional coal and iron mines under CF&I control. It was a daring gamble that Osgood ultimately lost; the expansion overextended CF&I financially, forcing Osgood and his associates to forfeit their control of the company. But the plan did succeed in substantially enlarging the Bessemer Works: of the $24 million invested in Osgood's improvement program, the lion's share went toward expanding and diversifying the Pueblo mill. Before, the facility had exclusively produced steel rails for train tracks, but by 1903 it was capable of manufacturing the full range of steel products. Renamed the Minnequa Works, the mill gave Pueblo its proud epithet:"the Pittsburgh of the West."[11]

Because the enlarged mill had a tremendous appetite for coal, CF&I's coal production tripled to 3.75 million tons annually—equaling almost half of Colorado's total output—between 1893 and 1903, the year the expansion was completed.[12] Although Osgood had navigated CF&I into dangerous financial waters to accomplish the expansion, business for CF&I and the state's other large operators was booming by the turn of the century. The *Denver Times* reported that "daily production of black diamonds now is considerably in excess of 30,000 tons, and coking ovens produce more than a thousand tons of coke for each day of the year."[13] CF&I's coal-mining operations at Sopris, Starkville, and Engleville employed thousands of men and were operating full-time. The Victor Fuels Company, one of CF&I's main competitors, had "an army of men" employed at its Hastings and Maitland mines, "and still," reported the *Times,* "the company finds it difficult to fill the orders it receives."[14]

The coal business was indeed booming, but not enough to lift CF&I out of the hole Osgood had dug in expanding the company. In debt to the tune of $7 million in July 1903, CF&I could not meet its obligations. Hard cash was the only solution, and to get it, CF&I's core coterie of stockholders had to relinquish their control of the company. They did so late in the summer of 1903, when a group led by John D. Rockefeller, Jr., put up the needed money. Osgood was pushed out, and for the next four decades CF&I would make up a small part of the Rockefellers' vast economic empire.[15]

Still, though it was small by eastern standards—or by Rockefeller standards—CF&I stretched over four western states and directly employed 15,000 people. At the time of the takeover, CF&I controlled twenty-three mines and nine coking plants in Colorado. About 6,000 men made a living digging coal and processing coke in the state, and another 6,000 toiled at the Minnequa Works. About 60,000 people lived on or near CF&I property. The high-quality beds of Las Animas County produced 52 percent of CF&I's coal, while Huerfano (20 percent) and Fremont (15 percent) counties contributed most of the balance.[16]

John C. Osgood had lost control of CF&I, but he rebounded quickly, taking over Victor Fuels. The new Victor-American Fuel Company soon became the state's second largest producer, with the Rocky Mountain Fuel Company close behind. Collectively, the three operators produced about 70 percent of Colorado's coal, with scores of smaller companies accounting for the remainder.[17] Following Rockefeller's takeover of CF&I, then, the overall management of the southern coalfields settled into a long period of corporate stability.

All told, in the relatively short span of thirty years, the coalfields of southern Colorado had been discovered, exploited, and consolidated in the hands of relatively few men. The growth of the industry was rapid and impressive, to be sure, but it also had its darker side: as elsewhere in turn-of-the-century America, the rise of the big corporation touched off violent labor struggles. The counterweight to the growing power of the corporation was the union, and for brief periods, at least, the union could have an enormous influence on the lives of miners and their families.

Local unions existed in Colorado as early as the 1860s, but not until the late 1870s did they begin affiliating with national labor organizations. A group of miners in Erie, in the northern coalfield, founded the state's first Knights of Labor assembly in 1878. In the ensuing years, the Knights' Colorado membership fluctuated. Numerous small strikes occurred, some meeting with success and others almost destroying the fledgling organization. The Knights' first real test came in August 1884, when the Colorado Coal and Iron Company ordered a 10-percent wage cut. Many miners rallied to the union's call for a walkout. Besides the pay cut, they objected to the company's practice of blacklisting union activists, its control over mining supplies, and its allegedly unfair methods for weighing coal (upon which miners' pay was based). These grievances, along with demands for union recognition, the eight-hour day, and pay for deadwork (meaning work other than coal- or ore-digging, such as laying track and shoring up overhead rock), would surface again and again in labor-management conflicts over the next five decades. The 1884 strike, which originated in Fremont County, quickly spread to the northern and southern fields, but the union was too weak to maintain a sustained drive. The historical record makes oblique reference to three hundred African American strikebreakers who were brought into the Walsenburg district from Tennessee; they were apparently the straw that broke the union's back. Miners reluctantly returned to work in December 1884, accepting the 10-percent pay cut.[18]

Though they affiliated with the Knights of Labor, the coal miners' unions of this era remained small, localized organizations with little cohesion or direction. A handful of union locals in Colorado's northern field banded together in 1886, forming the Coal Miners' Federation, but large-scale organization did not occur until the founding of the United Mine Workers of America (UMWA) in 1891. The UMWA would reign as the dominant labor union in the coalfields for the next forty-two years. However, even this organization attained only marginal success in unifying the state's coal miners.

From the time of the UMWA's arrival in Colorado in 1891 to the passage of the Wagner Act, which institutionalized collective bargaining in 1935, the miners' union had an erratic existence. To the coal miners and their families living in the camps, the union was like a comet. The majority of the time it was a small, mildly significant part of their lives. Yet when relations between labor and management became sufficiently tense, the union would come streaking back to the fore, championing the miners' demands for dignity and a better future.

Labor unrest erupted in Colorado's coalfields roughly every ten years, each time bringing violence and upheaval. In the months prior to these strikes, union membership would soar. Company spies would keep management informed of the increased union activity, and eventually the managers would exercise the unchecked authority they wielded over the residents of the company towns. Most typically, they would immediately fire any miner believed to be involved in union activity and expel him and his family from their company-owned house—sending them "down the canyon," as the saying went in the southern field. The operators flagrantly violated the miners' basic civil rights in other ways too, for example by prohibiting town residents from freely moving about, whether on or off company property, or by tampering with the U.S. mail—the post offices were usually located inside the company store and were thus managed as part of the company.

The big strike of 1903–4 typified this pattern: increased union activity, followed by draconian measures from the operators. At the end of 1902, the twenty local coal miners' unions in Colorado reported 2,470 members, but almost all of them were in the northern field, where greater ethnic homogeneity, a looser corporate infrastructure, and geography all worked in favor of unionization. In the southern field these same factors, especially ethnicity, all worked to the detriment of the union. A U.S. Industrial Commission report from the turn of the century clearly identified ethnic divisions as obstacles to miner solidarity:

> Were it not for the difficulties of language, the antipathy of race, and the jealousies of religion, the problem of labor organization would have been much easier, and organization would not have been delayed so long. But at the same time, it can not be said that these race problems are confined to foreign races. The jeopardy and defeat of the unions has been owing as often to the competition of unorganized Americans of native stock, in new fields, as in [sic] the competition of the foreign born.[19]

Only three locals existed in Colorado's southern field, at Pictou, Rugby, and Aguilar, and according to one historian, "these had no standing with the mine operators."[20] Toward the end of the summer of 1903, as the storm clouds gathered, the UMWA kicked off an immensely successful drive to organize the southern field. But management effectively counterattacked, firing and blacklisting union members, weakening the union substantially by the time the strike actually began in November. The UMWA District 15 secretary reported that over 8,000 men had been recruited to the union in the three months leading up to November, but that on the eve of the strike itself, "only 2000 remained in the union, over 6000 having been discharged and put on the blacklist."[21]

The strike continued on into 1904, but the operators maintained the firm upper hand, thoroughly extinguishing the short-lived burst of unionism that had spread through the southern field. One year after the strike began, only a hundred men in the southern field remained active in the union. The comet of unionism had streaked across Las Animas and Huerfano counties, and then disappeared, not to be seen again until the months preceding the Great Strike of 1913–14.

Many of the popular historians who have written about Colorado's southern coalfields portray the union as the paramount positive influence in the coal camps, as the righteous glue that bonded miners, their families, and their communities together. But this was generally not the case. While some, like the undertaker in Trinidad who only buried union men, did place the union on a high moral pedestal, many others were ambivalent, viewing the UMWA as only a small part of their lives.[22] One woman who grew up in the southern field remembers that a strong brotherhood existed among the miners, but adds that it had little to do with the union, because "at work, you know, some didn't like the union."[23] Even those who belonged to the UMWA were not necessarily active in it—or particularly enthusiastic about it. One miner's wife puts her husband in that category. "He keep his union up," she acknowledges, but he did so primarily to be on the safe side.[24]

Some of the techniques the union used to organize the miners could be as harsh as the measures the operators used to discourage solidarity. The so-called "active-passive" recruitment method, which the UMWA used to great effect in the months leading up to the Great Strike of 1913–14, was a case in point. The "active-passive" team consisted of two union miners. The active member would recruit conspicuously, talking openly with miners. Meanwhile, the passive member would seek work in the mines, feign anti-union sentiments, and often ingratiate himself to management as a company spy or "spotter." If the passive member found a miner receptive to his anti-union rhetoric, or alternatively if the active member came across a miner who refused to join the union, the passive member would report the miner to the company as a union *sympathizer*. Typically, the offending miner would be summarily fired—and replaced, unbeknownst to the company, by a *real* UMWA sympathizer. One source claims that in one month this technique resulted in 3,000 nonunion miners being released and replaced by union men. The UMWA placed twenty-one such recruiting teams in the southern field beginning in December 1912. By the following September, when the walkout began, almost the entire southern field had been organized.[25]

The union drew up seven demands justifying the walkout. The primary demand was that the operators recognize the union, and the next four called for miner-selected checkweighmen, pay for deadwork, a 10-percent wage increase, and the enforcement of mining safety laws. The sixth demand dealt specifically with the quality of life in the coal towns: the miners wanted "the right to trade in any store we please, and the right to choose our own boarding places and our own doctor." This demand—along with the miners' insistence that the company abolish the mine guard system, which imbued company-employed guards with the powers of law enforcement officials—testifies to the amount of control the company could wield over the lives of the miners and their families.[26] A poststrike government report succinctly stated the underlying issue. "The strikers passionately felt and believed that they were denied, not only a voice in fixing working conditions within the mines," explained the report, "but that political democracy, carrying with it rights and privileges guaranteed by the laws of the land, had likewise been flouted and repudiated by the owners."[27]

The Great Strike officially lasted from September 1913 to December 1914, when the union gave the order for its members to go back to work. In reality, the strike had ended months before, when many miners had returned to work in the aftermath of Ludlow, bringing coal production in the southern field back to prestrike levels. Ostensibly the strike had failed—the union was broken, and UMWA District 15 lay in financial ruins. On another level, though, the Great Strike brought substantial improvements to the area's coal mines and coal towns. As historian Donald McClurg writes, the strike's most important result was "the weakening of a system of paternalistic despotism."[28] The publicity surrounding the Ludlow Massacre, and also the evidence of corporate callousness that surfaced in the numerous hearings conducted after the strike, forced the operators to see labor in a more progressive light. In the end, the Great Strike and its aftermath brought about significant and far-reaching changes in labor-management relations, not just in southern Colorado's coalfields, but well beyond.[29]

CF&I's absentee owner, John D. Rockefeller, Jr., was the obvious lightning rod for public criticism, since he had been so far removed from the management of his Colorado properties. Rockefeller seemed genuinely alarmed by the course that events had taken in the coalfields, and especially by what had happened at Ludlow. As part of a public-relations campaign, he toured his coal properties in the southern field for two weeks in the fall of 1915. He visited a number of the company towns, attended a miners' dance, and even donned overalls and went into a mine to get a firsthand look at working conditions.[30] The primary purpose of Rockefeller's trip—photo opportunities aside—was to announce a new employee-representation program, called the Colorado Industrial Plan but more commonly known as the Rockefeller Plan. Designed to stave off any recurrence of the previous year's deadly and costly strike, the Rockefeller Plan reorganized CF&I into four districts and dictated that each district would in turn form four "Joint Committees on Industrial Relations," consisting of equal numbers of employees and managers. One committee in each district would address safety issues; the second would oversee sanitation, health, and housing; the third would take charge of recreation and education; and the fourth would govern industrial cooperation and conciliation. That two of the four committees were to address matters of a strictly community nature attests to the high priority miners placed on improving the living conditions in the camps.[31]

The Rockefeller Plan succeeded in improving safety conditions in CF&I's mines. As former camp resident Beatrice Nogare puts it, "after the 1913 strike [the miners] had rails and props where they worked." But the program also brought positive changes in camp life. According to Nogare, "What the strike won was all this freedom. [The company] had to pay money and not scrips. [So the miners] could go where they want to buy their stuff. That's what they won."[32] Likewise, miner Don Mitchell remembers that "after the 1913 strike, it got a little better all over. . . . [Rockefeller] said he don't know there was such conditions. Well, from then on, they changed it, see. They used to have nothing in these camps, see. Then [came] YMCAs and . . . showers and everything. Before there was nothing like that, see."[33] From Mitchell's perspective, the Rockefeller Plan improved both the way miners were treated and the way they lived.

"In these camps they built some homes," he explains. "Fix things up...and the men was treated much better."[34]

Still, despite some improvements in safety and camp life, the Rockefeller Plan was hardly the progressive marriage between management and labor that its namesake had hoped it would be. The plan ultimately failed because the company retained full control over the decision-making process. The labor-management committees could only recommend changes and thus lacked any real authority. As a result, the Rockefeller Plan, in the words of historian McClurg, became "less and less a method of sharing decision-making with the miner and more and more a means by which the will of the employer could be imposed without incurring the penalties of open industrial warfare."[35] By 1921 the plan was moribund.

Meanwhile, the union comet flamed out after the 1913–14 strike, just as it had after the 1903–4 strike. This time, though, the United Mine Workers of America would not return to the coalfields of Colorado until 1933, and only then under the protection of New Deal legislation. A combination of factors inhibited unionism throughout the 1920s, including a post–World War I recession, a nationwide surge of antiradicalism, the advent of union-weakening right-to-work laws, a marked decline in the demand for coal, and brutal infighting at the highest levels of the UMWA organization.[36] This is not to say that miners had no grievances in the 1920s—certainly they did. But they simply had no organizational vehicle by which to express them. The UMWA in Colorado was merely a "paper organization" by the mid-1920s, according to McClurg; it was "ill-equipped to contain, or even to influence, the stream of bitter protest that was shortly to flow. The time was growing ripe for the successful organization of the Colorado fields, but the union was not ready."[37]

Into this vacuum stepped the "Wobblies"—the Industrial Workers of the World, or IWW—to stage Colorado's last great strike before the era of institutionalized collective bargaining. As in earlier conflicts, a flurry of organizing activity occurred prior to the strike. The IWW began successfully organizing the coalfields in 1926, and in August 1927, Wobbly organizers called for a three-day walkout to protest the pending executions of Nicola Sacco and Bartolomeo Vanzetti, the Italian-immigrant anarchists who had been controversially convicted of murder in Massachusetts. The Wobbly organizers were surprised at the number of coal miners who responded to the call—1,132 of Huerfano County's 1,167 miners participated in the statewide protest.[38]

Inspired by this response, the Colorado Wobblies drew up a list of twenty-five demands, two of which addressed coal-camp life: "No increase in charges for rent and light in company owned houses" and "Labor organizers be allowed to come and go in company owned camps."[39] On October 18, half of the miners in the state struck under the IWW banner, with the biggest turnouts occurring in the northern field and in the southern field around Walsenburg. The four-month strike brought its share of violence to the state. Most notably, on November 21 police fired into a crowd of picketing miners at the Columbine mine in Weld County. The "Columbine Massacre" resulted in five dead and numerous injured. Throughout the strike, though, the Wobblies adhered to a nonviolent stance, which kept union-sponsored violence to a minimum.

The strike ended successfully in February 1928, when operators statewide hiked miners' wages. However, the State Industrial Commission judged that the miners' demands regarding camp life were unreasonable, reporting that company-provided facilities "such as stores, bath houses, [and] boarding houses . . . were all fair, adequate, and reasonable in price."[40] Today, the Wobbly strike of 1927–28 is best remembered for the Columbine Massacre, and for inspiring the progressive contract between the UMWA and Josephine Roche's Rocky Mountain Fuel Company. In the August 1928 agreement, Roche joined the union in asserting "that men employed are as much an essential factor in the industry as capital invested in it, and have rights in the determination of living and working conditions."[41]

Five years after the Wobbly strike, Congress passed the National Industrial Recovery Act of 1933, whose famous Section 7a guaranteed workers the right to select their own representatives in discussions and conflicts with management. Within weeks, the UMWA organized Colorado's miners in one grand sweep. Only then did it establish itself as a more permanent and pervasive presence. All told, the UMWA's trajectory in southern Colorado is probably best summed up in the prosaic words of miner Don Mitchell. "I'll tell you when the mines got organized really. They was never organized here.... What I mean, [they] never got nowheres until [Franklin] Roosevelt, when they gave you the right to organize, see....They never had the union down in this part until then."[42]

## Chapter Two
# The Company Town

*Mostly out of need, but partly from paternalistic motives and
occasionally because of avarice, the operators established
company stores to sell groceries, clothing, and other items;
obtained doctors; and otherwise attempted to establish the
essentials of community life.*
—U.S. Coal Mines Administration, 1947[1]

Company-owned coal-mining towns began to dot the landscape of
Huerfano and Las Animas counties in the 1880s. The Denver & Rio Grande
Railroad, through its Coal and Town Company subsidiary, had already set
up a variety of company-run communities as the main line pushed south.
Colorado Springs, for example, was originally a wholly owned company
town established a few miles outside the existing settlement of Colorado
City. There was no independent municipal government; the D&RG had
complete control over the layout and management of the new settlement.
The constant buzz of activity surrounding the new town naturally lured
businessmen, and Colorado Springs quickly eclipsed and eventually swal-
lowed up Colorado City. The D&RG employed a similar tactic in Pueblo,
creating the town of Bessemer, and in Trinidad, where it founded the town
of El Moro five miles northeast of the existing plaza village.

So with some experience behind it, the D&RG began in the late 1870s
to establish towns for the sole purpose of digging and processing coal.
Apparently hard-pressed for an original name, the company opened the El
Moro mine four miles southeast of Trinidad (and six miles south of the
town of El Moro) in 1877. By the end of the following year, 180 coke
ovens were operating at the site, and a town had been erected to support
the miners and coke workers. This community would soon become known
as Engleville or simply Engle.[2]

More towns followed. Starkville was established five miles south of
Trinidad in 1879. Morley was founded in 1882, just a few miles north of
the New Mexico border on Raton Pass. Sopris, four miles west of Trinidad,
was platted in 1888. These towns all fell within a short five- or six-mile

radius of Trinidad, which was beginning to prosper as a mining and rail service center. Five miles does not seem like a great distance by today's standards, but in the 1870s, before the advent of the automobile, it was too far to commute. Towns had to be established right at the mines in order to support a labor force with limited mobility.[3]

By the end of the 1880s, company towns were popping up on the rich coal beds north of Trinidad. Twelve miles from the plaza city, Forbes came into existence in 1889, as did Hastings, the first operation in Berwind Canyon, twenty miles to the northwest.

In Huerfano County, the need for the coal companies to erect towns was initially less acute, since Walsenburg sat right atop a great north-south seam that stretched for fifteen miles on either side of the town. Coal was being mined one mile west of Walsenburg, in what would eventually become the huge Walsen mine, as early as 1876. But production was limited at this early stage, and miners simply commuted from town. The county's first dedicated company towns appeared toward the end of the 1880s. Pictou, two miles north of Walsenburg, and Rouse, five miles south, were both founded in 1889.[4]

Despite the severe nationwide depression that began in 1893, southern Colorado's company towns boomed in the ten years following the 1893 merger of the Colorado Fuel Company and Colorado Coal and Iron. During this decade, the newly formed CF&I grew from 10,000 to 15,000 employees, about 40 percent of whom worked in the Pueblo steel mill.[5] By 1903, the industrial infrastructure required to mine, process, and transport southern Colorado coal was firmly in place. In Las Animas County, the towns of Primero (1901), Segundo (1901), and Tercio (1902) were founded in the Purgatoire River valley. Rugby (1900), Tabasco (1901), and Delagua (1903) joined the expanding operations in Berwind Canyon. In Huerfano County, Maitland (1898), Pryor (1898), Hezron (1902), and Walsen (1902) were also established during this period of growth (see figures 2 and 3).[6]

About half of southern Colorado's coal camps were "closed," meaning that the operating company owned virtually all the property and all the buildings. The other half were considered "open" or "partially open." Geography usually dictated whether a town was open or closed. "Open" towns were those located close enough to existing noncompany towns—Trinidad, Walsenburg, Aguilar, or others—that the operators did not have to supply all the necessities of life for employees living there. Rouse, Walsen, Robinson, and McNally, all within a couple of miles of Walsenburg, were

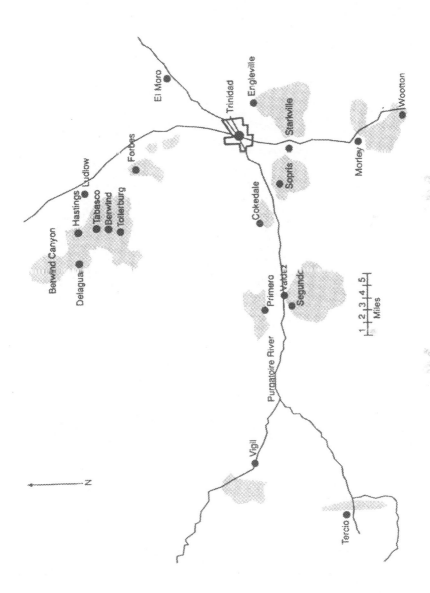

Figure 2. The Coal Towns of Las Animas County

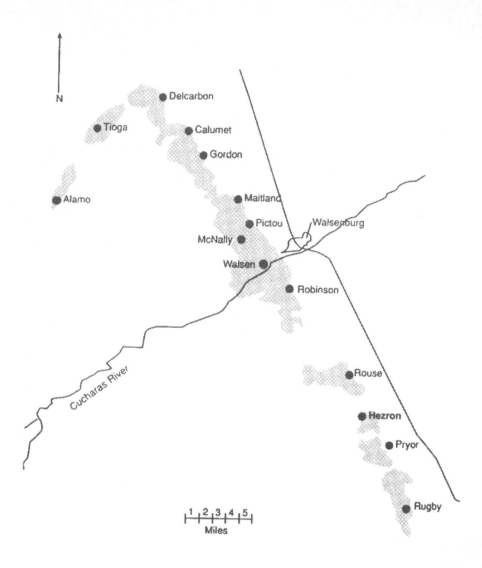

Figure 3. The Coal Towns of Huerfano County

open camps. Morley, Tercio, Primero, and Segundo, with more remote locations, were closed.

The towns built around the turn of the century, especially those constructed during CF&I's period of expansion from 1899 to 1903, were markedly different from those built earlier. To a great degree, the early towns were ad hoc operations, as the company had not yet developed a comprehensive strategy for managing growth or providing services. The quality of life in these earlier towns often depended on the demeanor of the town superintendent, who was the company manager responsible for overseeing the mine and the surrounding settlement. A good superintendent, for example, might enforce high standards of sanitation and ensure that home repairs and general upkeep were given priority. To many superintendents, though, the town was an afterthought—a distraction that took valuable time and money away from operating the mine. Given that production and profitability were the measures of success, the well-run, sanitary town was probably the exception prior to 1900.

Historian Crandall Shifflett has suggested that the American company town went through three phases of development. The first was a pioneer or frontier stage beginning in the 1880s and lasting roughly until World War I. The second was a paternalistic phase that lasted until the Great Depression. The third phase was marked by the decline of the company town, ending sometime in the 1950s.

Southern Colorado's coal towns fit nicely into this three-phase model—in concept, at least, if not in timing.[7] Like Appalachia, southern Colorado had its "frontier" phase before the turn of the century. During this period, many of the region's coal miners were of northern European extraction. To use Shifflett's description of their Appalachian counterparts, these early miners were "single or unattached males who had been uprooted from definite expectations of social behavior," and who "sought relief in exaggerated and sporadic outbursts of unbridled" activity.[8] Such men typically felt little stake in any sort of long-term community. But while this transient "frontier" phase may have persisted in Appalachia until World War I, in southern Colorado it was clearly coming to an end at the turn of the century. The profile of the region's average miner began to change in the late 1880s and 1890s, as southern and eastern Europeans entered the coal mines in large numbers. Many of these immigrant miners either brought family with them or worked to raise enough money to bring relatives over.

The paternalism Shifflett found in Appalachian company towns after World War I came earlier to the southern Colorado coalfields. We can date its arrival to July 25, 1901, the day CF&I created its Sociological Department. Born in the wake of a 1901 strike, the Sociological Department operated until 1915, when camp management was reorganized under the Rockefeller Plan. The department was a remarkable attempt to redress the social problems that contributed to discontent and labor unrest. CF&I management gave the Sociological Department a sweeping, open-ended mission: it took "general charge of all matters pertaining to education and sanitary conditions and any other matters which should assist in bettering conditions under which our men live."[9] Dr. Richard W. Corwin, who had long been the director of CF&I's medical programs, was named the first superintendent of the new department. He initially employed a full staff of about two dozen people, approximately half of whom taught in the camps' kindergartens and grade schools.

From 1901 to 1904, the Sociological Department published *Camp and Plant*, a biweekly company newspaper that educated employees and their families about company operations and kept them up-to-date on various social and cultural activities in the camps. *Camp and Plant* also reported on the Sociological Department's progress in the five areas for which it was responsible: education, social training, industrial training, housing, and communications. The department was ambitious, to say the least. In its first year alone, it took charge of employee housing and established public schools, reading and night schools, and kindergartens, while also launching a variety of other programs, including cooking classes, traveling libraries, lecture series, and social organizations, including boys' and girls' clubs.[10]

But while the Sociological Department was ambitious, it also had an erratic history. Between 1901 and 1908 it made substantial progress in improving camp living conditions. It achieved a remarkable level of consistency in camp management and quality of life, and it fulfilled its highest priority by implementing a regimented, company-wide approach to schooling. But in 1908, the department experienced a reversal of fortune when Lamont M. Bowers was appointed manager of CF&I's Colorado operations. Bowers would later achieve infamy as the implacable executive who was largely responsible for provoking the violent Great Strike of 1913–14. Soon after his appointment to CF&I's top Colorado spot, Bowers sharply curtailed the Sociological Department's activities; he saw the services it offered to the camp dwellers as unnecessary frills. Under his direction, the department's ambitious programs were underfunded or terminated, and camp living conditions steadily declined, ultimately helping spark the Great Strike.[11] In the strike's wake, as part of the Rockefeller Plan, the Young

Men's Christian Association (YMCA) assumed many of the Sociological Department's former responsibilities, reinvigorating to some degree the corporation's commitment to employee welfare.

CF&I's Sociological Department was a curious experiment in labor-management relations. In one sense, the agency stands as evidence that CF&I was genuinely concerned about employee well-being. But the efforts of the Sociological Department were not just an extended exercise in altruism. They sprang even more from considerations of expediency. Because the coal towns were so isolated, CF&I management realized, the corporation stood nearly alone as the dominant influence over the lives of workers and their families. Such influence gave CF&I an opportunity to mold its work force as it saw fit—and specifically, to ensure that camp residents would always act in the best interests of the company. It was this goal, more than any altruistic impulse, that drove the Sociological Department.[12]

In retrospect, CF&I's Sociological Department stands as the most tangible example of corporate paternalism, a concept that conjures up conflicting images of guiding benevolence and calculated control. In those places where there was no existing town, a coal company had to provide services—social institutions, recreational facilities, health care, schooling, housing—that would normally fall outside the corporate domain. But inevitably, when a company got involved in all these areas of life, it gained a great deal of control over miners and their families. Paternalism was a carrot, necessary to lure and maintain a stable work force. It "was simply another cost of doing business," as historian Shifflett puts it. "It had to be paid if a company wanted to remain competitive."[13] But paternalism was also a stick. The company could deny its workers basic living necessities on a whim, for whatever political or economic ends it saw fit. Paternalism, mused the federal Commission on Industrial Relations after the Great Strike, "raises the question of whether or not political liberty [is] possible in a community where every man's livelihood depends on the good will and the favor of a handful of men who control his opportunity to work." Reviewing the events of the Great Strike, the commission offered an answer to its own question. "Experience in the Colorado coal camps...," it concluded, "proves that all the safeguards yet devised for the free exercise of the popular will are futile to prevent political domination when corporations or individuals control absolutely the industrial and economic life of the community."[14]

In the actions of the Sociological Department, then, company benevolence and company control went hand in hand. The same held true for virtually any service the corporation provided to camp residents. For another example, consider the handling of law-and-order affairs. In southern Colorado, company-employed camp marshals were deputized as sheriffs, authorized to enforce the law and restore peace in times of disturbance. Given the camps' rugged, isolated setting, such an arrangement was necessary; there was simply no other entity present to wield legal authority and enforce order.[15]   But the arrangement also gave enormous power to the company.  The deputized "peace officers" were paid directly by the company, and rather than exercise their authority impartially, according to the dictates of state and local law, deputies exercised authority according to the best interests of the corporation that cut their paychecks.  This method of keeping the peace was most twisted during times of labor unrest, when hired mine guards—often the employees of a detective agency under contract to the mine operators—were commonly deputized as officers of the law.

The same contradiction between corporate benevolence and corporate control also applied to the operation of company stores.  More than any other single element in company towns, the company store has come to represent the pervasive power of the paternalistic employer.  "I owe my soul to the company store," that famous refrain from Tennessee Ernie Ford's "Sixteen Tons," has become part of American folklore.  Ford's lyrics seem to capture the archetypal plight of the miner:  his vulnerability before faceless corporate oppression, his spiritual struggle to maintain his identity, his hopeless toil for a better life.  Oral histories of southern Colorado are replete with references to "that Tennessee Ernie Ford song" and claims that "it was just like that."

But this is an instance of life imitating art.  A corporation like CF&I could indeed use company stores to wield power over its employees.  But Ford's song neglects to mention that the company stores, like the company-paid "peace officers," were something of a necessary evil.  They were the only means of ensuring that the miners and their families would have access to food, supplies, and the other necessities of life.  As historian Price Fishback has pointed out, a mining region like southern Colorado was generally remote and lightly populated, so it had few existing stores.  Moreover, independent entrepreneurs were usually reluctant to move in and open stores once mining began, since the industry was notoriously unstable and the future business decisions of a mining company were unpredictable. Finally, most mining towns were too small to support a profitable store.[16] With independent entrepreneurs unwilling to assume these risks, it was left to the mining company itself to establish and operate a store. Here the company provided everything miners and their families needed, from gunpowder, picks, and shovels to dry goods, furniture, and animal feed.

Historians have frequently portrayed the company store as a nefarious vehicle of corporate oppression. The company, according to the most familiar versions, paid the miner in scrip redeemable only at the store, forcing the miner to pay the store's grossly inflated prices. This forced the miner to draw credit at the store against his next puny paycheck, plunging him ever deeper into arrears. The company reaped great profits from this arrangement, while the miner was consigned to a life of debt and indenture—so the story goes.

But evidence indicates that the relationship between the miner and the company store in southern Colorado's coalfields did not readily conform to this model of deliberate economic enslavement. In Colorado, the store was part of an economic package that included wages, living arrangements, and other forms of employee compensation. With well over two dozen mines operating in southern Colorado and northern New Mexico, the operators were constrained by competition amongst themselves, and as we will see in chapter 4, there was a high degree of employee transience in the fields and a general shortage of labor at most times. The operators generally could not afford to squeeze a miner at the company store because a disgruntled miner usually had the option of picking up and moving to another company's mine. Consequently, as Fishback has argued, limits on store prices "were imposed by competition among mines to attract laborers to their towns."[17]

Also, even though the coalfields were geographically remote, the company stores still faced some degree of competition from independent stores in nearby "open" towns. About half of CF&I's stores, which were operated by the company's Colorado Supply Company subsidiary, had independent competitors.[18] In 1914, John C. Osgood, the president of the Victor-American Fuel Company, testified to the effects of such competition. "Most of our mines are near enough to some town," he noted, "so that once a week or so the men can go to town and trade....The maximum amount of our sales at any time has not exceeded 25 per cent of the payroll, so that it does not look like we are forcing our men to make all their purchases at our stores."[19]

The company store in southern Colorado, then, was more of a necessary service to employees than a weapon for corporate control. Still, the same paternalistic contradictions that were built into the use of deputized "peace officers" were also built into the operation of the company store. As with the deputies, the stores became another weapon for controlling workers' behavior during times of labor-management tension. The operators could rescind credit at the store, and they could fire and blacklist miners for shopping in noncompany stores. And of course, fired miners and their families were also evicted from their company-owned houses and forced to look elsewhere to live. As former camp resident Steve Surisky puts it, "You trade [at the company store] or else...down the canyon you would go."[20]

Evidence suggests that such draconian measures were primarily invoked during the weeks leading up to a strike, when both the union and management were maneuvering for maximum control of the miners. Beatrice Nogare, whose father worked in numerous mines around Trinidad from the turn of the century up to 1913–14, recalls that the pressure to buy at the company store was particularly intense just before the Great Strike. As Beatrice remembers it:

> We had to buy everything at the store....The pay was in scrip money, this was before the strike....You couldn't go to Trinidad to buy anything....If anybody would go down...and buy something in Trinidad, if the superintendent found out next morning they would have their check time hanging on the hook, instead of the check number they carry into the mine....They would have to move away from there, no more work for them there. That was pretty tough for it was hard to get another job right away.[21]

Not just strikes but also other conditions—such as times when the company was experiencing an overproduction of coal or a labor glut—could strengthen the operators' hand and enable them to force miners to shop at company stores. According to miner Frank Gutierrez, much depended on the temperament of the superintendent. "A lot of fellas had farms close to the camp and they raised vegetables....They sell goats, they sell cheese...," Gutierrez recalls. "If the superintendent wanted to buy cheese, he buys it [and the peddler] could go in there day and night if they wanted to." But, he adds, "some superintendents didn't like that....They wanted you to trade at the company store."[22] In some conditions and under some superintendents, then, the company store could take on the coercive qualities that have made such stores so notorious.

One other service that reflected the two contradictory sides of paternalism was company housing. The companies provided homes for miners and their families, and by the turn of the century much of this corporate-owned housing was comfortable, sturdy, and reasonably priced. But this ostensibly altruistic and practical act of providing a decent place to live was also a primary source of instability in the miner's life. The company could deny the shelter of a home almost instantaneously if the miner engaged in some activity—either on the job or in his personal life—that seemed to conflict with the interests of the company. The miner and his family could be rendered homeless in a matter of days.

Especially in times of labor strife, this threat was the miners' Achilles' heel. "[The miner] loses his right to the home both for himself and his family when he loses or gives up the job," explained a 1925 government study. "In times of industrial disturbance especially, men have not dared to look elsewhere for work, fearing that their families would be evicted if the companies discovered that the tenant miners had gone in search of other employment."[23] Similarly, in 1947, the U.S. Coal Mines Administration's "Boone Report" found that a miner in company housing was typically given no more than five days to vacate after dismissal. Rents were often excessive compared to local conditions, and maintenance and other basic landlord responsibilities were usually not specified in the lease. Company housing arrangements, the report charged, were "more reminiscent of feudalism than characteristic of the mutual dignity and independence in present-day business contracts."[24]

Still, regardless of the lopsided lease agreements, housing in southern Colorado's coal camps stabilized at the turn of the century. CF&I's four-year expansion and the creation of the Sociological Department coincided fortuitously and resulted in the construction of new camps that were better designed and built than the old ones. The camps built in this period were some of CF&I's largest. A total of more than 500 new homes went up in camps like Primero (200 homes), Segundo (75 homes), Hezron (75 homes), and Tabasco (40 homes).[25] All of these camps had modern conveniences, including electricity and piped-in water, available from hydrants for fire protection and domestic use.[26]

However, the coal towns were extremely homogeneous in their appearance. When historian James Allen wrote his stark description of a generic western company town, he might just as well have had the southern Colorado camps in mind:

> Certain general features usually stood out. First to be noted would be the standard, uniform architecture of the company owned houses. In a

prominent location, however, would stand a larger, more imposing structure: the home of the superintendent....The town seemed to center around
a focal point where a store, community hall, school, and other public
buildings were located. The company store usually dominated the group.
It would be noted that the settlement had no "suburbs," or no gradual
build up from a few scattered homes to a center of population. Rather,
one would note the complete isolation of the community and the defi-
niteness of its boundaries. Finally it would be apparent that the existence of the community was completely dependent on a single enter-
prise, because a mine...would seem to dominate the entire scene.[27]

Historians writing on labor-management relations commonly criticize these
camps for their monotonous appearance, with the same house design re-
peated row after row. The communities were indeed unattractive in many
cases, but the monotony was largely dictated to the company by simple
economies of scale. The quickest, most cost-effective way to provide housing for a growing population was to repeat a few basic designs, thereby
simplifying the planning and construction process and reducing design and
materials costs.

The camp houses constructed by CF&I in this period and later were
mostly three- or four-room structures, although a number of six-room dwellings were also built. The majority of these houses were built of concrete
blocks or wood-framed, with the typical four-roomer costing $700 to build.
The company rented homes for $2.00 per room per month, with water
furnished free, except at Frederick and Segundo, where the company charged
25¢ per room. The miner paid 35¢ a month for each electrical outlet in the
home, and $1.50 to $2.00 per ton of coal for heating and cooking.[28]

The Sociological Department had a say in making these dwellings as
attractive and comfortable as possible. As Dr. Corwin wrote in the
department's first annual report, "Not only have the inside comforts of the
buildings been considered but as well the outside appearance, and the moral
effect of architecture and paint not overlooked."[29] *The Denver Post,* track-
ing the progress of construction, lauded Corwin's efforts. "The houses are
three, four, and six-room structures, built on stone foundations, lathed and
plastered, each having porches and all painted and quite neat and attractive in appearance," reported the *Post.* "The occupants are all furnished
pure mountain water at their doors free of cost."[30]

While the input of the Sociological Department did improve housing,
the harsh realities of mining-camp life could not be mitigated by "moral"

architecture and a fresh coat of paint. The houses were built in a tight radius around the mine and the processing facilities associated with it. With noxious, foul-smelling gases belching from coke ovens and the like, living in such a setting could be harmful to one's health. It could also be offensive to one's sense of cleanliness and aesthetics. Given southern Colorado's semi-arid climate, most of these communities were devoid of any trees or landscaping, and the streets were unpaved. Keeping a house clean was a constant losing battle against mud, grime, and coal dust.[31]

The quality of life in coal-camp housing was not solely dependent on the operators, although large corporations were often in a better position than smaller companies, from the standpoint of capital costs, to build and maintain quality housing. The personal habits of tenants and superintendents often influenced livability more than any other factor. The 1947 Boone Report found that "There is patently a close relationship between maintenance and housekeeping by tenants. Houses kept in good repair by Management are likely to be well-kept and neatly furnished by the tenants." But, the report added, "many exceptions have been noted, where dilapidated structures were handsomely equipped with furniture and modern electrical appliances....In other instances virtually new houses were almost bare inside, with beds in apparently permanent disarray, unwashed dishes on tables, garbage on the floors, and foul odors permeating every room."[32]

Bob Tapia, who worked in a half-dozen camps in Las Animas and Huerfano counties, liked the American Smelting Company camp at Cokedale the best because the superintendent there ensured that the settlement stayed livable. "They kept it real nice," Tapia recalls of Cokedale. "We had a superintendent that was really rough on people if they didn't keep it nice. He went around and inspected the yards and if they were full of weeds he'd tell them to cut them, and if they didn't cut them he'd send a man to cut them and then he'd charge it to the people. Well, he wanted a clean camp and...he had a nice beautiful place."[33]

The cleanliness of the coal camps was more than just an aesthetic concern. Unsanitary conditions could also pose a real threat to human health. A number of government studies conducted during this period show that sanitary conditions varied greatly among the nation's coal camps, even within a specific region. Again, the management practices of camp superintendents came into play, but geographic factors were also important. The Boone Report pointed out that "water supply is a more serious problem in the far West than in the eastern or central mining regions" simply because there was so little of it. As a result, the report observed, "Rivers in the bituminous-coal-producing [western] areas are heavily polluted with sewage, impurities, and mine wastes of all sorts. Mine water...has introduced a relatively high percentage of sulfur, plus calcium, iron, and other minerals. Animals kept on the watershed have contributed to the problem."[34]

Tributaries of the Purgatoire and Cucharas rivers, which supplied water to many of the mining communities around Trinidad and Walsenburg respectively, were hardly suited to the region's domestic and industrial needs. These rivers and creeks were taxed to the point where human health was affected. *Camp and Plant* advised its readers on a number of occasions to boil any drinking water taken from these rivers. "Typhoid fever is putting in its appearance," one issue warned, "and everyone ought to drink boiled water."[35]

Sewage disposal was an even more acute problem affecting sanitary conditions. In 1920, a sample of 811 coal-mining camps nationwide found that just over 20 percent had running water, only 3 percent had bathtubs or showers, and less than 4 percent had flush toilets; outhouses were the norm in almost 61 percent of company towns. Twenty-six years later, a similar study showed that little had changed; this larger sampling found that 88.4 percent of company-owned homes still relied on outhouses and only 5.2 percent had integrated sewage systems.[36] The problems caused by such primitive methods of sewage disposal could be severe. "One privy more or less faulty in construction or lacking in care is neither a pleasant nor healthful adjunct to a farmhouse," the 1920 report allowed, "but hundreds of such marplots within an area of a few acres will well-nigh submerge all other assets of home and community livability, to say nothing of imperiling the health of every person who lives or labors within reach of the privy emanations."[37]

Based on today's knowledge of disease and toxicity, we must assume that the health of camp residents suffered from such conditions. The byproducts of mining and coking coal only exacerbated the situation. One former resident of Cokedale remembers the smell that would descend on the town whenever the wind blew in the gases from the coke ovens. "We didn't call it smog in those days; we just called it bad smoke," he says.[38] A 1903 issue of *Camp and Plant* resorted to shades of Orwellian doublespeak in describing the situation in Starkville: "The coke ovens, which have been closed for sixty days, are again running at full capacity, and our citizens really enjoy the clouds of smoke which cover our town."[39]

Such strained euphemism makes it clear that even at the turn of the

century—long before the Great Strike and the Rockefeller Plan that marked
the pinnacle of corporate paternalism—CF&I knew that living conditions in
the camps presented a serious public-relations challenge. It was the Progressive Era, a time when Upton Sinclair and other "muckrakers" were busy
digging up the dark side of all American industries, including coal. Coal-
camp life at the time was not the living hell some writers have claimed, but
it was also far from ideal, and it could hardly be called democratic. Even
the sunny prose of *Camp and Plant* couldn't hide this reality.

Indeed, whenever CF&I responded to critics of camp conditions, it inad-
vertently acknowledged that serious problems did in fact exist. In October
1903, for instance, *Camp and Plant* felt obligated to respond to "some 'hot
air' artist" who had written a *Denver Post* article excoriating CF&I's treatment of its workers. *Camp and Plant* paraphrased the accusations—"that
the miners of southern Colorado were making only starvation wages and
never saw any cash, receiving all their earnings in scrip"—and then went on
to ridicule the *Post* critique, retorting that it "sounds laughable to those on
the ground who know the conditions as they really exist."[40] Perhaps a
rebuttal like this reassured the friends of CF&I. But since rebutting the
charges compelled *Camp and Plant* to repeat them, such an exchange inevitably gave air to concerns about the ways miners and their families were
being treated.

Sometimes defensiveness and fear of the muckrakers crept into corporate propaganda even when no specific charges had been leveled. A 1901
*Camp and Plant* piece on the company town of Sopris, for example, ex-
alted the camp's "picturesque location"—and then, tellingly, saw fit to add
that "The person who only knows 'camps' by hearsay...would be surprised."
If a "reporter for a yellow journal" or "a photograph fiend" were to visit
Sopris, continued *Camp and Plant,* they "would find their mission
objectless....Their imaginations would have to supply the requisite lurid
'copy' for the facts show an entirely different state of affairs from that
published in the 'penny dreadfuls.'"[41] Public-relations prose like this, while
self-congratulatory, also betrayed an unmistakable and uneasy defensiveness. CF&I seemed haunted by the hobgoblins of its anticorporate critics,
both real and imagined. Even in the immediate absence of negative publicity, the company could sound downright paranoid of what a potential de-
tractor *might* say.

■

Just as the contemporary criticisms leveled by muckrakers haunted CF&I, the later writings of many labor historians loom ominously over our image of southern Colorado's coal-company towns. We tend to see these towns as hellish places to live, as places where the corporation ruled over workers and residents with an iron fist. And it is undeniably true that, in the case of company housing and company store policies, the power of the company could indeed eclipse the power of the law—and that the consequences for workers, especially in times of labor unrest, could be severe indeed.

But in the final assessment, this bleak picture oversimplifies and some-what distorts the realities of working and living in these towns. If there were factors that militated against democracy in the camps, that under-mined residents' autonomy and left them vulnerable to the whim and will of the corporation, there were also other factors that mitigated the harsh-ness of company-town life. In particular, the company recognized it could not earn a favorable bottom line unless its workers were reasonably con-tented. That was the primary rationale behind the founding of CF&I's Sociological Department, and more than any other entity, the Sociological Department improved living conditions in the coal towns. In doing so, it also set the standard that other companies had to follow if they hoped to compete successfully for workers. Every operator knew that, if a miner and his family grew disgruntled with camp conditions, they usually had the option of moving to another camp in the region. In general, then, the need to maintain a stable and productive work force kept the coal companies from going too far in their efforts to control or subjugate their employees. And so a tense and tenuous balance—built on the unstable foundation of corporate paternalism—existed between the operators and the residents of the camps.

# Life in the Camps: Images

**Above:** Miners, lunch pails in hand, pose for a portrait after a day's work.

**Left:** The opening of the Muir mine.

**Above right:** An extended mining family in Las Animas County.

**Right:** The town of Hastings. As was typical in company towns, housing was erected in the midst of the mining operations.

**This page:** The towns of Rouse (**top**) and Morley. The Morley company store is at upper left in the bottom photo.

**Facing page, from top:** Italian coke pullers at the coke ovens in Tercio, and (**inset**) the Tercio company store. The company town of Sopris, before and after CF&I's building program (1901–4); Sopris photos by O. E. Aultman.

**This page:** North Starkville, with Fisher's Peak beyond (**top**).
Starkville students pose with their teacher in 1886; photo by E. G. Hower.

**Facing page:** The mine at Primero.

This page: The Ludlow tent colony before the fire (top), and a Red Cross team visits the scene after the tragedy (center). Bottom: In 1910, a Primero mine explosion killed more than 100 men. Here, camp residents await news of friends, husbands, and fathers.

Facing page: Hungarian miners serve as pallbearers for a countryman killed in the Primero blast (above); the Hungarian miners and their families bury five casualties of the blast in the Catholic cemetery in Trinidad.

*Chapter Three*

# The Community

*In spite of idiosyncrasies of individual settlements, nearly all
residents of coal towns shared some common modes of
thought, habits, prejudices, values, aspirations,
and experiences.*
—CRANDALL SHIFFLETT, HISTORIAN[1]

*Once you're a coal miner, you're just as friendly
with one guy as the other one.*
—JOHN VALDEZ, COAL MINER AND CAMP RESIDENT[2]

*It's the closeness of the people, closeness of the miners. And
something about camp life...after you moved out you miss
what you had there, because people were so close.*
—CAROLINE TOMSIC, CAMP RESIDENT[3]

In the coal camps of southern Colorado, people forged communities under
dramatically different circumstances than they might have faced in a more
typical American small town. Coal towns were isolated, populated largely
by immigrants, and driven by a dangerous activity—mining coal. These
characteristics colored all relations among camp residents and contributed
to a shared sense of community. The omnipotent corporate presence, the
geographic isolation, and the ubiquitous danger of mining combined to
give the coal miner and his family a very different experience from their
relatives who settled in large cities or established smaller towns. Still, while
life in the camps might not have been "typical" in a broader American
context, it was usually all that recently immigrated residents had ever known
of the United States. To the miners, the company town—with all its ex-
tremes—was America.

Ethnic diversity was the most conspicuous social characteristic of the
coal communities. And in general, the pressures of camp life had a positive
influence on ethnic relations. The camps" often harsh environment compelled ethnic groups that had a long history of animosity to learn to live
and work together peacefully. Greeks and Bulgarians, Croats and Slovenes,

Italians and Tyroleans buried their mutual animosities and were able to forge communities. Doing so was a necessity. The dangers of coal mining and the whims of coal-town management required that miners and their families develop a support system independent of the company. During periods of labor strife, the union performed this function, but as noted in chapter 1, these periods were relatively short, and the union was absent from the miners' lives most of the rest of the time. Religion might have provided a communal bond, but like so many other institutions of town life, the church was closely tied to the company. Miners and their families usually preferred to worship individually or to associate with independent churches outside of company control.

A sense of community could not be imposed from above. It was created and maintained by camp residents, who relied on it for defense against the company, against isolation, and against the traumatic nature of mining coal. Community solidarity evolved in the context of camp residents' everyday activities and social interactions—in their ethnic relations, their health care practices, their religious beliefs, their leisure pursuits. The sense of community was one of the few elements of camp life that the residents themselves could control.

Coal camps became cohesive communities in large part thanks to dramatic demographic shifts that took place between 1890 and 1910. Before 1890, miners tended to be single men with little interest in forging communities or putting down roots. Later immigrants, though, either brought their families with them or sent for them as soon as financially possible. In 1915, John C. Osgood, then president of the Victor-American Fuel Company, testified to this trend. "In years gone by most of our men were English-speaking men," he explained. "Now they are mostly foreigners—almost from every land....They have relatives in the camps....The majority of these men come out here to stay."[4] By 1900, a high percentage of coal-town residents were women and children. Jesse F. Welborn, president of CF&I, indicated in his testimony before a federal commission in 1914 that the ratio of family members to miners was about three to one. For example, he stated, the camp at Primero had 225 to 250 men, which "would mean 600 people" in the camp. At Tercio, Welborn testified, CF&I had "100 people working for [the] company" with 300 total in the camp.[5]

Changes in age, gender, and marital status between 1890 and 1910 accompanied another crucial demographic shift in the southern Colorado coal camps: a trend toward greater ethnic diversity. Prior to this period, English and Welsh miners—men who had been trained as miners in the old country—had made up a large portion of the work force. Hispanos, including those who came from the villages around Trinidad and Walsenburg and those who migrated seasonally from northern New Mexico, also comprised a large percentage of mine labor in this early period. A smattering of southern European and Slavic miners were also present, but only in relatively small numbers.[6]

The accompanying graphs (figures 4, 5, and 6), drawing on census data taken from 1880 to 1920, show the dramatic demographic changes that occurred in Huerfano and Las Animas counties around the turn of the century. Between 1890 and 1910, southern and eastern Europeans, and especially Italians, arrived in droves, markedly changing the ethnic composition and atmosphere of the camps. By 1910, an impressive 17.6 percent of the residents in these counties were natives of southern or eastern Europe. The vast majority of these new immigrants settled either in or close to the coal camps.[7]

By 1900, two-thirds of CF&I's 9,000 coal miners were immigrants from southern and eastern Europe. In all, thirty-two nationalities were represented on the company's payroll, and twenty-seven different languages were spoken in the camps. Well over half of these nationalities were actually subjects of the crumbling Austro-Hungarian empire, and they were often

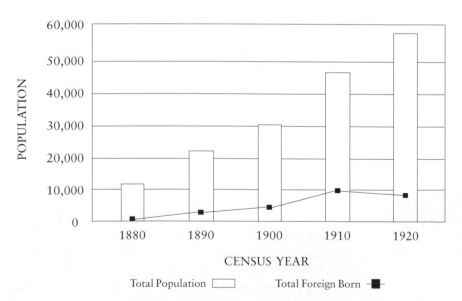

Figure 4. Combined population of Las Animas and Huerfano Counties.

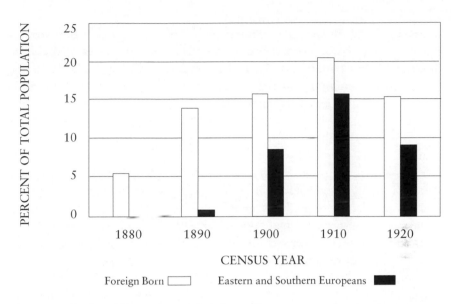

Figure 5. Ratio of Eastern and Southern Europeans to foreign born as a percentage of total population in Las Animas and Huerfano Counties, 1890–1920.

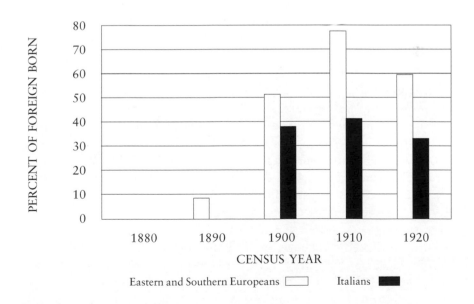

Figure 6. Ratio of Italians to total foreign born in Las Animas and Huerfano Counties, 1900–1920.

lumped together under the catchall category of "Austrians." But without question they considered themselves distinct nationalities. Magyars, Slovenes, Poles, Croats, Bosnians, Ruthenians, and Moravians—to name just a few—poured into the region, and they were joined by Greeks, Russians, Spaniards, Germans, Japanese, and Irish. Italians were by far the largest single ethnic group in the field, outnumbering "Austrians," the second-largest nationality, by a factor of four to one at the outbreak of World War I.[8]

The ethnic mix in the camps also included African Americans, Hispanic Americans, and Mexican nationals. Blacks were on the payroll in numerous camps. At one time, the mine at Morley employed thirty-nine African Americans, and Berwind had eight to ten black families. Hispanos had worked the mines since operations began in the 1870s, and they composed 15.63 percent of the total work force in Las Animas in 1915.[9]

The operators believed that such a diverse ethnic mix worked in their favor, and evidence indicates that they tried to manipulate ethnic and language differences to discourage worker solidarity. Lamont M. Bowers, CF&I's Colorado manager in the early 1900s, admitted that the company consciously mixed nationalities, so that "when too many of one nationality [got] into a given district...[CF&I] would go adjust their men so that no very large percent in any mine could communicate with the others."[10] This idea—using the barrier of language to inhibit worker unity—was well known, but as we will see later in this chapter, the operators' attempts to use ethnicity to drive miners apart was largely unsuccessful.

It is true that residential segregation by ethnicity was the norm in the camps, with the best housing going to Anglo-Americans and northern Europeans. Blacks and Hispanos lived in designated areas, as did southern and eastern Europeans. Many, if not most, chose to settle in neighborhoods with others of their ethnic group.[11] Martha Todd grew up in the camps and remembers most of them being segregated by ethnicity and nationality. "People segregated themselves, nationally...," she recalls. "The Germans stayed with the Germans. The Italians stayed with the Italians. The different Slavic people stayed with their own."[12] These various ghettos usually carried distinctive, often derogatory names. In Dawson, just over Raton Pass in New Mexico, blacks lived in "Coontown," Greeks lived on "Number 4 Hill," and Italians lived in "Laredo." The camp at Delagua was also separated by race and nationality, with blacks living in "Uptown," Austrians in "Bricktown," Italians in "Cast Town," and Japanese in "Japtown."[13]

Camp segregation was largely a function of immigration, of newcomers to a strange land seeking out people like themselves. The tendency was perpetuated to some degree by word of mouth. An Italian, for example, would send news of employment opportunities back home to relatives and friends, who would then come join him. In this way, certain nationalities became prevalent at certain camps. Walt Laney remembers that Welsh and Irish gravitated to Pictou and Maitland outside of Walsenburg, while Germans clustered at the Denaley mine and Slovenes were dominant at Gordon.[14]

For a new immigrant, southern Colorado's coalfields were a stark and daunting place. The immigrant, male or female, often made the two-month trip from Europe alone and faced a strange land, language, and culture. Those who came over at the urging of a friend or a relative who was already established in a camp had it a little easier, since the acquaintance could serve as a mentor of sorts. Regardless, the trauma of immigration was acute, the loneliness and homesickness wrenching. Initially, many hated their new home.

Unlike many of his fellow immigrants, Ed Tomsic did not come to America for political or financial reasons, but his sense of fear and alienation upon arriving was just as strong. "I left Europe because my folks wanted me to become a priest, and I run away from there," he explains. "It took me 38 days on a boat until we get to Trinidad and Engleville. I started work. I was a little over 18. Believe it or not, I cry many, many times, why did I come? My hands was full of blisters." The only thing that kept Ed in America was his refusal to admit he had made a mistake. "They wasn't poor my folks," he says. "[They] want to send me the money to go back, but I had too much pride to go back."[15]

In 1920, seventeen-year-old Maria Batuello came by herself from the Tyrol, the Alpine region that is now split between Austria and northern Italy. Maria's aunt and uncle had arrived a year before and urged her to come, luring her with the promise of good marriage prospects in the camps. But Maria found it difficult to adjust to America. She remembers her despondent state of mind: "I was hurt. I don't like it here. I cry and cry. I don't know nobody except my uncle and auntie, but even them I don't see them for a long time..., and I cry and I tell you one thing, if the way wasn't with the sea, with the water, I walk home."[16]

Many women followed their husbands to southern Colorado, usually coming separately once enough money could be saved for the trip. Besides the upheaval of leaving home and enduring an arduous voyage by steamship and train, the women arrived with no knowledge of local customs, which often caused as much stress as the actual physical dislocation. Al Berte remembers his mother insisting that his father put curtains in the back of his 1920 Chevrolet when he picked her up at the depot in Walsenburg. She did not want people to see her because she was embarrassed that her only dress was too old-fashioned.[17]

Angela Tonso's fiancé worked for a time in the coalfields before returning to the Tyrol in 1913 to marry her. The newlyweds arrived back in Walsenburg on September 10, just ten days before the Great Strike began. After working for a week at Rouse, Angela's husband struck with the rest of the miners, was arrested on a picket line, and spent four days incommunicado in the Trinidad jail. Angela, who spoke no English, had no idea what had happened to her husband during those four days. As far as she knew, he had simply disappeared. After just two weeks in the new land, Angela Tonso had had enough. "Oh, I was ready to go back home," she recalls. "I says, if this is America, I don't want any part of it."[18]

Immigrants had to overcome the language barrier if they were to function and survive in the camps. Learning the language often meant being resourceful. Gertrude Ferraro claims she mastered English in six months by "looking at the funnies and reading *The Denver Post*." Some immigrants had an easier time of it than others; children, in particular, tended to pick up English more quickly than adults. Nick Halamandris, son of Greek immigrants, grew up in the camps during the 1920s and was able to pick up "a little Japanese, Italian, Spanish, French, and Slavic [languages]..., and of course Greek too." His introduction to a language usually began with the profanities because, as he explains, "that's what a kid learns first." Italian immigrant Al Berte recalls learning English much more quickly than his two older sisters, and his parents struggled for years with the language. "They had an awful hard time trying to go out to the store, and trying to buy things, trying to express what they wanted," Berte says. "They mostly had to point at different things."[19]

Adapting to life on the rugged industrial frontier of a foreign country was certainly traumatic enough. But for many camp residents, the trauma was exacerbated by racial or ethnic tension. The tense and dangerous work of mining coal, the economic hardships, and the sporadic attempts to unionize the miners all offered opportunities for racial or ethnic animosity to boil over. One former deputy sheriff in Huerfano County remembers that when miners had run-ins with the law, more often than not they sprang from ethnic disputes. Many fights were sparked by nationalistic grudges brought from Europe.[20]

Ethnic animosities could spill over into workplace disputes as well. For example, a frequent source of controversy was the assignment of checkweighmen, or miners who were responsible for weighing their fellow workers' coal cars at the end of a day to determine how much each man should be paid. As John C. Osgood, president of Victor-American, told a congressional committee, "It is right difficult for these men to agree on a checkweighman; if they agree on an Italian, the slavs believe he is stealing from them and giving to his Italian friends, and if it is a slav it is vice versa."[21]

Racial divisions were, if anything, even sharper and more embittered than those between European ethnic groups. Racism against nonwhites seems to have been the norm in Cokedale, the American Smelting Company town ten miles west of Trinidad. Cokedale had a very active chapter of the Ku Klux Klan in the 1920s that staged numerous cross-burnings on the hill above town. Even worse, the Klan's activity may have had the tacit support of the company. For instance, a number of miners recall an unwritten company rule that blacks were not to be hired. "They just wouldn't hire them," says Frank Wojtylka. "You never saw a colored man working here in this mine. You did at Valdez....They work in CF&I [mines] and Sopris and places like that," but not at Cokedale.[22]

Asians, mostly Japanese, were rarely accepted as equals in the mining communities. Stark cultural differences fueled the fires of racism, but the Japanese aroused even more resentment because they often arrived in the southern Colorado fields as strikebreakers, and hard feelings remained long after the strikes ended. Thirty-two Japanese strikebreakers arrived in Walsenburg during the 1901–3 strike after being "roughly handled" in Fremont County coal mines. The union, the United Mine Workers of America, saw the Japanese as a threat and excluded them from the organization because they knew many miners would refuse to belong to any union that had Asian members. In Cokedale, the large Japanese work force was kept completely segregated both above and below ground. Japanese workers had their own bathhouse and a separate entry into the mine; as one miner puts it, "there was just Jap people working in there and a Jap boss."[23]

Many Hispano miners and their families also faced discrimination. While Hispanos were not ostracized to the extent that the Japanese were, they were also not fully accepted into the European-dominated community structure. European miners typically viewed Hispanos much as they did the

Japanese: as frequent strikebreakers and as a cheap source of labor that undermined the other workers' efforts to secure a fair wage. The operators sought to take advantage of this tension by hiring more Hispanos. That Hispanos were drawn to coal mining's relatively good wages is without question. As a farm laborer, a Hispano could earn about one dollar a day, but a miner could more than double that income, earning about sixty dollars a month. From 1900 to 1910, 11,000 Hispano New Mexicans—men, women, and children—migrated to southern Colorado to mine coal or provide support services to the growing industrial population.[24]

To be sure, Hispanos were at least partially integrated into the mining communities, and they coexisted peacefully with Europeans in some camps. At the Tollerburg, Valdez, and Ramsey mines, where the work forces were not solidly Hispano, Hispanos were nevertheless elected as union delegates, and at Pryor and the Ludlow tent colony, Hispano committeemen served during the Great Strike.[25] But in other camps the populations did not mix. For example, Louis Guigli remembers that "All could go to dances in those days, Slavs, Polish, English, and Irish people. But they would never let a Spanish [Hispano] inside the dance hall...because they didn't want the Spanish people to mix with the Italians because every time they came in there was a lot of trouble and fighting. Guns were pulled and everything else. They couldn't mix with them because they couldn't get along with them."[26] Similarly, Clarence Cordova recalls that as a child he was shunned by other Hispanos because he hung around with Slavic kids. "See, the little Mexican town was from up the creek and the American one was this way, and when they came together they always fought," Cordova explains. "Well, I lived in the company's house and I went with George Duzneack and the Mexican kids didn't like me."[27]

Some Hispanos lived in company housing, while others lived in the numerous adobe plaza villages that dotted southern Colorado and northern New Mexico. The operators found this autonomy somewhat disconcerting and typically viewed the Hispanos as "clannish." The plaza village served to some degree as an indigenous support structure, so it reduced company control over this large portion of the work force.[28] Furthermore, members of the Anglo power structure often misunderstood Hispano culture. For example, when Hispano workers at Forbes skipped work to observe a day of mourning for an infant who had succumbed to disease, the superintendent assumed the workers had gone out on strike. After the circumstances were explained to him, the official derisively asked, "What am I to know of your heathenish customs?"[29]

There can be little doubt that Asians and Hispanos were excluded from or only partially integrated into the coal-camp community. But it would be a mistake to view the camps as seething caldrons of racial and ethnic hatred. The majority of the European ethnic groups, at least, lived in relative harmony, bolstering each other in their larger struggle for survival and economic prosperity. Many immigrants found the coal-camp communities to be full of sympathy and sharing, and many of the oral histories collected from former camp residents echo the theme of ethnic harmony and collective support.

Two factors in particular provided the glue that held these communities together: the shared immigrant experience and the shared rhythms of life in a coal camp. Many immigrants had been subjected to political or economic oppression in their native lands, all had weathered a long voyage to an unknown land, and all experienced the harshness of laboring in the burgeoning industrial era. "We were all in the same boat," remembers Angela Tonso, "poor the same. There wasn't any jealousy or hatred."[30] The shared odyssey, combined with the exigencies of mining coal—the danger, the toil, the exploitation—gave camp residents a strong sense of commonality. The community felt both respect and sympathy for its individual members, and these sentiments mitigated the nationalism and ethnocentrism that might have otherwise divided many of the Europeans.

Certainly, immigrants carried varying degrees of nationalism and chauvinism to the New World, and the camps were far from an ethnic utopia. Still, a strong air of tolerance did exist. Ann Laney recalls that "We were closely knit, far more than you are in town. Everybody knew each other and got along real well....It seems like they accepted you when you moved in. There was no difference. And really, I think all nationalities got along real good there in the coal camps."[31] Italian immigrant Louis Guigli has similar memories. "Where we lived there were Italian and Polish people," he says. "Everybody was real friendly. Everybody would go and visit one another....Everyone pitched in and drank wine, whiskey, and pitched food together and had a good time. There was no enemy living in those days....Everyone appreciated one another."[32]

According to Hispano miner Gerardo Tovar, divisions between camps were more significant than divisions between ethnicities. Groups of men from different camps got into brawls fairly frequently, and Tovar remembers that his non-Hispanic friends in the Dawson camp would stick with him in such a fight, even against other non-Hispanics. In such situations, loyalty to one's fellow camp members outweighed any ethnic divide.[33]

The same could not always be said of the divide between blacks and whites; as we have seen, there was widespread exclusion of African Americans by other groups in the coalfields. Still, interracial relations were not universally strained. According to some old-time residents, blacks and whites mixed harmoniously. Alfred Owens, an African American miner who spent his entire life in the Walsenburg area, insisted that he never experienced prejudice in the camps. "You know, I was raised up around white people and I can't remember no prejudice...," he says. "We played ball together, we went together....In all the mining camps practically everybody's the same....We didn't have no Jim Crow stuff like that."[34]  White miners remember it the same way. For example, Dan Desantis, who had black neighbors in Berwind, recalls that "We didn't see no difference....They [his neighbors] was good people."[35]

One key element that did much to encourage attitudes of tolerance in the camps was the dangerous nature of mining coal. Perhaps all professions develop a sense of brotherhood or sisterhood, but the especially enormous hazards that came with mining forged a particularly strong bond among miners, regardless of race or culture. Miners knew that the best way to mitigate the mine's ubiquitous danger was to work together and look out for each other. This approach transcended ethnic distinctions and other divisions that might otherwise separate miners on the surface. As miner John Tomsic suggests, the men were "so close together in the mine [that]...one was watching the other one, protecting the other guy all the time..., and any danger that would come up...it just drawed the men right together."[36]

Such cooperation was not limited to an underground setting. The miners' families also recognized the logic of mutual support. Each morning, women and children said good-bye to their fathers, sons, brothers, and husbands, knowing full well the dangers the men would face that day in the mine. Every day, women went about their work wondering if their men would emerge from the mine alive and unhurt. Knowing the mine could indiscriminately kill their loved ones, erase their means of survival, and shatter their lives was an oppressive emotional burden. But family members could derive some comfort from the companionship of others facing the same horrific possibility. By collectively facing the prospect of losing a husband, a father, or a son, camp residents ended up bridging some of the ethnic or racial divides that might have otherwise come between them.

To be sure, moral support from friends and neighbors was not in itself enough to help a miner and his family overcome severe injury or disability.

Here was one crucial area where management stepped in to lend a hand. Most mining companies in the West provided some level of health care to their employees, particularly in the area of industrial medicine, the treatment of injuries or ailments resulting from actual mining activities. Providing medical care was not just a matter of altruism on the company's part. Given the inherent dangers of the industry, the larger employers had to provide medical service in order to attract and maintain work forces. In the coal industry, health care was funded through a prepayment plan under which a small sum, on the order of one dollar per month, was deducted from a miner's pay. A survey conducted in the 1940s showed that 81 percent of the miners working in the coalfields of southern Colorado were covered under this type of plan—a much higher percentage than in other mining regions. Southern Colorado was also different from other coal regions around the country in that this single monthly checkoff also covered hospital services.[37]

The relatively advanced state of industrial medicine in the Colorado coalfields can largely be attributed to CF&I's Medical Department. This agency was headed by Dr. Richard W. Corwin, the same man who headed the company's Sociological Department, and a fair amount of overlap existed between the two entities. Corwin established the company's first medical services in 1881, when CF&I was still the Colorado Coal and Iron Company, and he remained in charge of medical services for forty-eight years until his death in 1929.[38]

Corwin began dispatching physicians to the coal regions in 1882. Initially he assigned one doctor to Trinidad and one to Walsenburg, but as operations expanded he assigned each camp its own doctor. Most camps' medical facilities consisted mainly of a well-equipped doctor's office. The camp physicians were paid a salary and usually received housing and domestic coal free of charge. Their duties were broad; they provided "gratuitous services for all cases except those of confinement, venereal diseases, and fight bruises."[39] The physicians would treat these ailments as well, but the patient was required to pay a fee above the monthly charge.

To pay for pharmaceuticals, each camp physician was given a monthly allowance of three cents for every miner or dependent under his charge. Most of the time this allowance fell far short of what was needed. In the typical camp, it amounted to only twelve dollars per month for drugs, and a doctor usually distributed twenty-five dollars' worth of medication during any given month. The balance had to be made up from the for-fee services he provided or from private practice he conducted on the side.

In oral interviews, former camp residents speak highly of the company doctors and their dedication to duty. Ann Laney, who grew up in the mining towns, remembers that the doctor "used to come out to the mines, and he would make his calls at the mines, and then he would go out in the different neighborhoods."[40] Miners would report sick family members to the mine office in the morning, and the doctor would usually make his rounds by early afternoon.

Along with medical services in the camps themselves, CF&I also operated a large medical center in Pueblo that served the workers in the Minnequa steel mill and the severely ill and injured sent from the company's camps. Camp residents with ailments that could not be treated locally were taken to the Pueblo facility free of charge. Opened in 1882, the hospital was initially a modest thirty-bed facility, but in 1902 the company expanded the complex into a state-of-the-art medical center comprising thirteen buildings on twenty acres of land. Known as Minnequa Hospital, the facility was staffed by nine physicians and surgeons and five interns—numbers that testify to just how hazardous the coal and iron industry was. CF&I also established a nursing school in 1899 as part of its hospital services.[41]

But the formal medical facilities and programs established by CF&I and the other large coal companies were only part of the miners' health care picture. Typically, the mining communities' more mundane medical needs were met by herbal remedies, home cures, and other forms of folk medicine that the different ethnic groups had brought with them to southern Colorado. Residents used folk remedies for everything from preventing the common cold to setting broken bones and delivering babies. References to this type of medicine appear frequently in the oral-history records, suggesting that its use was common and widespread. One former camp resident, when asked to describe the variety of home remedies that were common knowledge, answered that "There was so many I can't remember them all."[42]

Miner August Andreatta recalls that the remedies the immigrants brought from the old country were augmented by the local folklore of southern Colorado. "There was some herbs, you know that come from the old country, teas and stuff like that," Andreatta explains. But he also remembers that his mother used herbal remedies that she had learned from an elderly woman who was part Native American. "She showed my mother a lot of these herbs that were out in the prairie," says Andreatta. "I remember she used to pick a weed that was called La Aranja De San Jose in Spanish. The branch of St. Joseph, and you boil a couple of little branches in water, and drink the water and it physics you like that. If you need a physic, see, everything would come out."[43]

Herbal remedies like this one were common in the camps. Alfred Owens's mother was probably typical of many. "She used to get different herbs from the hills and make teas," Owens says. "She used to get weeds and things like that and make some kind of medicine tea." Some coal-camp people used chamomile tea as a cure-all for minor ailments, and Cora Hribar remembers drinking a terribly bitter wild sage tonic for three weeks every spring "to purify the blood." Garlic was also used to cure various problems, including worms, and according to Louis Guigli garlic was a sure-fire way to prevent the flu. "My mother made a necklace around our neck with pure garlic," he recalls, "and we never did get the flu in our family, and in later years we learned why, because nobody wanted to sit by us."[44]

In addition to herbs, miners and their families used a variety of other home remedies, including a strong dose of whiskey and a variety of snake oils delivered to remote locations by "the Raleighman." Lard, in various forms, could perform minor miracles. Once again, Louis Guigli explains its use:

> My mother had old lard rendered and let it get real old, so it would get good and green and real old, and it would take out splinters. She would put it on our chests so we wouldn't catch cold. And beat up wine and eggs and drink it, and also boiled wine and cloves and take it and go to bed, and in the morning we got up as good as new.[45]

Just as miners and their families maintained their physical health through a combination of institutional medicine and home remedies, so also they looked after their spiritual health through a combination of formal religious institutions and independent worship. Religion was an important part of a mining family's life. Although the operators attempted—somewhat meekly—to provide for the spiritual needs of camp residents, company-sponsored religious activities generally failed. Frequently, residents sought religious guidance in Walsenburg or Trinidad or simply provided for their own spiritual needs.

The diversity of religious beliefs in the camps paralleled the diversity of ethnicity. Italian immigrants and Hispanos were generally devout Catholics, while eastern European immigrants were Catholic, Protestant, or Russian or Greek Orthodox. But no matter what the church, it is safe to say that religion was a major influence in the mining communities. "Church was first. Then school," says Ed Tomsic. "But church, on a Sunday, before noon and afternoon....Most people was awful religious....Sunday was church."[46] Contemporary observers noticed the importance of religion too. An 1899 article in the *Denver Times,* for instance, enthusiastically declared that "it is doubtful if there is another coal mining region in the United States, if in the world, in which the same high order of morality exists as in the camps of this territory."[47] Hyperbole aside, it is true that church activity boomed in Colorado's coal-mining region at the turn of the century, undoubtedly driven by the local population growth that began in the 1890s.

The operators either built dedicated houses of worship, which were available to all denominations, or opened other camp facilities, such as schools and recreation halls, for religious uses. Primero, which was established in 1901 at the height of CF&I's experiments in industrial sociology, had a dedicated church built in 1903. Protestants and Catholics shared the structure, and in the interest of making the most of the building, the basement was used for club and lodge meetings, reading, and other uses.[48] To tend to the morality of the young, CF&I also ran Sunday schools—"particularly [in camps] that are located at a distance from communities that are provided with those facilities," according to a congressional committee.[49]

Although most camp residents held religion to be an important part of their lives, religious practices had to be adapted to the special conditions that existed in the camps. Historian David Corbin, writing about the coal camps of the East, believes that "traditional religious identifications" were upset by the "industrial capitalism of the coal fields and company towns." According to Corbin, "while the religious traditions that the immigrants brought with them were quite strong, their traditional religious institutions were weakened or altered."[50] Corbin's thesis holds true for the coal towns of southern Colorado as well. The corporate influence in church affairs greatly altered the relationship between clergy and parishioners.

Just as the company could supersede the law through its control of housing, mail, and daily necessities, so also it could eclipse the clergy in religious matters. This was particularly true in the closed camps. The operators wanted to meet the spiritual needs of their employees, but they also worried that the church might become a rallying point for dissent. The church had a potentially powerful political element to it, since it adjudicated regularly on issues of morality. Religious orders often espoused political beliefs far to the left of what was acceptable to the company, and a preacher could agitate a congregation with a single sermon.[51] To forestall dissent, then, the companies typically kept the church on a short leash. With regard to religion, one CF&I official told a federal investigatory commission, the miners had "just what the Company furnished them. No one can go in there [church] without the consent of the Company..., religious or otherwise."[52] The church at Primero, for example, was paid for and maintained by CF&I, and management refused to allow anyone to use it for potentially inflammatory activities.

When spiritual and corporate interests clashed, the company, having the political and economic upper hand, always prevailed. Not surprisingly, this corporate hegemony over matters of faith was most apparent during periods of labor strife. During the 1927 Wobbly strike, for instance, the Federal Council of the Church of Christ reported that "The rank and file of churches, ministers and church members seemed to be largely uninformed [about strike issues] and lacking in conscience on industrial problems. In many churches, the employers' point of view is the dominant influence." In CF&I's closed camps, the council charged, "the activities of church representatives are entirely subject to the wishes of the mine superintendents."[53]

The company's tight control over religious institutions created a credibility gap between camp residents and the camp church. As a result, most residents either sought affiliation with churches outside the camps or tended to their own spiritual needs. The baptism of Emma Zanetell's newborn children was a case in point. Due to high infant mortality, it was risky for a parent like Emma to make the trip to town and wait for a formal, priest-administered baptism. But going to the company-run church right in camp apparently did not strike Emma as a desirable option either. So she turned to female friends and relatives to perform the baptismal rites.[54]

CF&I's Sociological Department seems to have recognized the tenuous relationship between corporate-sponsored religion and camp residents. Professing to be "perfectly non-sectarian in dealing with people of various faiths," the department essentially washed its hands of church affairs.[55] "The Sociological Department," according to the agency's annual report for 1904–5, "conducts no direct religious work, not because we undervalue the importance of such work in any community, but because we feel that this branch of welfare work can be much better left to the...churches." This policy left local CF&I managers to handle religious matters as they saw fit.[56]

Like religious practices and health care, leisure and recreation became a matter of company control on one level, but a source of autonomy and community solidarity on another. Camp administrators tried to provide residents with leisure and recreational opportunities, but these were strictly activities in which the company wanted the miner to engage. Moreover, recreational diversions were an additional expense for the company and were the first to be eliminated during economic downturns.

In CF&I's camps, the company administered a number of simple recreation-oriented programs, including libraries, reading rooms, traveling lecturers, and night schools. *Camp and Plant* frequently highlighted these amenities in its descriptions of camp life. Most company-supported leisure options had a strong assimilationist undertone. The reading room at Sopris, for example, stocked periodicals that reflected "mainstream" American values: *Success, The North American Review, American Boy, Everybody's Magazine, Frank Leslie's Popular Monthly,* and *The Ladies' Home Journal,* just to name several.[57] It was very much in the company's interest to mold a compliant, passive work force, and corporate-sponsored leisure outlets like the Sopris library clearly tried to promote this goal.

Another amenity the company offered, the night school, was meant to achieve the same end. According to the company's perspective, miners should be hard-working and loyal, wives should be supportive (which entailed running the home efficiently and making it a pleasant place to be), and children should be groomed as the next generation of upstanding miners and miners' wives. The night school program reinforced all of these values with classes on civics, homemaking, English, and hygiene. Children's schooling (which will be discussed in chapter 6) further reinforced management's idealized view of industrial life.

Camp schoolhouses often doubled as community centers, where dances were held on Saturday nights and movies were shown on occasion. The company also operated saloons in some camps, but saloons did not fit in with the moral lifestyle the company was trying to promote. Alcohol use was an ongoing problem for the operators—one they could never truly control to their satisfaction.

Camp residents seem to have engaged in the company-provided leisure activities with a moderate level of interest. CF&I's Sociological Department recognized that "there is little in the way of diversion" in the camps and experimented in 1902 and 1903 with an "entertainment course," featuring regional entertainers who toured six of the company's camps. The entertainers included a lecturer, an impersonator, a contralto singer, and a pianist. The response to the tour was encouraging, and the department recommended "a more extensive series of entertainments for the coming year, covering a greater territory and including a greater variety of talent."[58]   There is no evidence that the company adopted this recommendation, however.

Saturday night dances—whether on company property or in private halls—were extremely popular among camp residents.  Often the whole camp would attend, "from the brass up to the cokeblower."  In Pictou, dances were held on the top floor of the schoolhouse, and the residents of Cokedale turned the town bar into a dance hall when prohibition was passed in Colorado in 1918.  Miners' benevolent and fraternal societies frequently banded together to sponsor the dances: *Camp and Plant* reported on a masquerade ball in Starkville in 1903 that was cosponsored by the local Knights of Pythias, Odd Fellows, and Red Men.  A dance like this one was an important diversion that residents, after the toils of the work week, enjoyed immensely.  As *Camp and Plant* said of the Starkville ball, "a glorious good time was had by all.  A good crowd was present, including many from Trinidad.  The hall was crowded to its fullest capacity.  At midnight the lodge members' wives served delicious refreshments.  It was an early hour when the crowd dispersed."[59]

Music at these events, supplied by bands from Walsenburg or Trinidad, often echoed the traditional folk melodies of the various ethnic groups, played on guitar, violin, and accordion.  Frank Gutierrez reminisces, "We'd say 'let's hire the pushy-pulley' [accordionist] and he played all night....He played polkas, waltzes and cunas....We all had a lot of fun, old people, young people."[60]  Many former residents fondly recall a black piano player from Trinidad named Sonny "Sunshine" Williams who was always in demand for dances.  "He never had a music lesson in his life," says Martha Todd, "but he could play the piano for dancing."[61]

If camp residents enjoyed dances at night, they just as eagerly embraced baseball by day.  Given the local terrain, baseball diamonds were difficult to build and maintain.  But all the same, baseball was the main pastime during the warmer months and was played at all different levels in the camps, from children's pickup games to semipro traveling leagues.  The sport was an important part of camp life because, as Clarence Cordova explains, it was "the only entertainment there was.  Oh, a circus would come once in a while.  But baseball, that's all there was going on every Sunday."  Similarly, Ann Laney says that baseball "was the most popular [game] and everybody would play.  The whole group would come together—men, women, children, boys, and girls."[62]

Each camp in the region had its own team, and many had two—a first- and a second-string squad.  In fact, if a miner could play ball, it often improved his chance of employment. "Well, if you was a ball player you'd get a job. They always wanted good ball players," remembers Clarence Cordova.[63] People gathered on Sundays to watch the games, and local rivalries were fierce. Wagering on the outcome was common. *Camp and Plant* dedicated up to a quarter of its pages to reporting on the weekend games, giving extensive line scores and statistics. The descriptions could be quite colorful, capturing the excitement and enthusiasm camp residents held for the game. "On account of an error in the first inning the visitors succeeded in running in one score," said *Camp and Plant* of one 1903 contest. "Had it not been for this it would have been a shut-out, as their stick work was sadly deficient. They had the bases full, and had a good chance to make a few runs, but the man at bat wasn't there with the goods."[64]

Evidence indicates that immigrants picked up on the enthusiasm for baseball and formed ethnically based teams. Clarence Cordova organized a Hispano team at Pryor—but he laments that he had to include "a couple of slavish [sic] kids" on the roster "in case somebody got hurt." He remembers walking all the way from Pryor to Walsenburg once to see a supposedly all-female team called the Bloomer Girls play the Walsenburg nine. "Everybody wanted to see the Bloomer Girls play and come to look at it, [but] they was all men," he laughs. "You could tell they had wigs on. There was only two women, the rest was all men. But I'll tell you they sure made fools out of Walsenburg."[65]

Camp superintendents actively recruited good ball players—ringers—from other teams and throughout the region. These players were given the best or easiest jobs at the mine, since they were kept on the payroll primarily to play ball.[66] The American Smelting Company once "shipped in" a ringer for their Cokedale team and gave him a house—"painted and cleaned and everything"—that two families had been living in, recalls Emilio Ferraro. This type of special treatment could understandably be the source of hard feelings, and Cokedale's ringer "couldn't get along so good with some of the men" in town.[67]

For all the fun of baseball games, dances, and other activities, perhaps the most popular leisure pursuit of all was simply to socialize with friends. As Al Berte remembers, "what people did mostly...is visit one another."[68] By today's standards such an activity may seem banal, but in the era before the widespread availability of automobiles and radios, simple socializing was an economical and pleasant way to spend time and an important element in strengthening a sense of community. According to Alfred Owens,

"You could have more good times in the camps than you could coming into town."[69]

Through visiting, residents could relax, exchange news and gossip, and get to know each other better. Historian Crandall Shifflett believes that simple visiting was crucial for maintaining the "instrumental relationships" that helped residents survive in the tension-filled coal-camp environment.[70] The reminiscences of the coal-camp residents bear out Shifflett's observation. Al Berte, for one, tells how visiting helped to establish relations of reciprocity. "It was nothing for my mom to buy a ham and in the evenings go and visit this family...," he remembers, "and then maybe two or three nights later go visit somebody else and they'd come to your home."[71] Ed Tomsic explains how a simple visit could turn into a party. "On Saturday," he says, "first thing we go in one house or another house, roll the linoleum and move the furniture and start pulling [i.e., drinking] and dancing."[72] Gertrude Ferraro holds similar memories. "There's some people that had...outside ovens," she recalls. "They make these great big nice loaves of bread and people were very friendly and very easy to get along with..., no matter what kind of nationality you was....And somebody'd know how to play accordion. [We would] take the furniture out of one room and we'd dance all night."[73]

Picnicking was the warm-weather counterpart to visiting. The terrain and climate of Las Animas and Huerfano counties were well suited to outdoor activities, with mountains, streams, and forests all within easy access of most of the camps. A number of springs and campgrounds were located in the vicinity of the Spanish Peaks. Louis Guigli's family would go up there many weekends. "We would take the whole family up to the mountains on Saturday and Sunday all in one bunch," says Guigli, "and we'd have a good time playing boccie, cooking, and having a good time with all the rest of the Italian people in the neighborhood."[74]

Sulphur Springs, a campground up the Cucharas River valley, was especially popular. In addition to family outings, large community-scale events were frequently organized. "They told us we couldn't use the Local money [i.e., union funds] for the picnics," recalls Ed Tomsic, "[but] we did just the same. I always said that nobody can stop us. That's our money, and we are going to have it. Sure, all the kids, children, miners, everybody went, and we had a very nice time."[75]

When not attending dances, ball games, or picnics, camp residents gravitated to Walsenburg and Trinidad, which offered city-style attractions and were probably quite colorful and exciting compared to the general monotony of camp life. On Saturday nights neither town slept. Simply "going into town" became a social event in itself. Shops stayed open late, and people would carpool, ride the streetcar, or walk to the city to take part of the action. Residents of camps in the Purgatoire Valley could catch the "Dago Flyer" train that ran twice a day from Trinidad, and for twenty-five cents there was an interurban trolley that ran from Cokedale to Trinidad every two hours from eight o'clock in the morning until midnight.[76] "Everyone came in for groceries, a nip, and a dance," says Glen Aultman, a lifelong resident of Trinidad. Mining-camp residents were joined by ranchers and townsfolk. Trinidad was "a hustling, bustling hub of activity around the wholesale district," remembers Aultman. "On Saturday evenings the sidewalks were so full that you could hardly walk. It was just like during a parade, pretty near every Saturday afternoon, winter or summer."[77] Miner Don Mitchell has similar memories of Walsenburg: "Couldn't walk the street on a Saturday night it was so crowded," he says. "Had more people in the middle of the night than they do now."[78]

Hearing such recollections of life in southern Colorado, it becomes clear that the coal-company towns were hardly the oppressive, draconian work camps we are often led to believe. It is true that residents faced the real dangers of mining and the challenges of living in a remote and isolated region. But these shared pressures compelled them to built mutual support systems and create tightly knit communities—communities that often transcended ethnic divisions. Despite the company's efforts to control residents, the camps were alive with traditional ethnic religious practices and collective leisure pursuits. Residents even exercised autonomy by using traditional folk remedies in their health care. The coal-company towns were no paradise on earth, to be sure, but many people recall the camps being pleasant places to live. And many of these same people, after moving out, found that they missed the neighborly closeness and the strong sense of community that were such a vital part of coal-camp life.

# Chapter Four
# A Miner's Life

*They feel in digging coal a stirring challenge from Nature—a pitting of human skills against the resistance of the earth.*
—U.S. COAL MINES ADMINISTRATION, 1947[1]

*The mine has been good to me and it's been bad to me....My back's been broke and my neck's been broke from rock falls.*
—ALFRED OWENS, COAL MINER[2]

*The family had no picture of him and the body was not mutilated. And so the family wanted a picture. . . . My father would pose the family around the body and the undertaker would open the eyes, and my father would take the picture.*
—GLEN AULTMAN, TRINIDAD PHOTOGRAPHER[3]

Life in the coal camps, as we have seen, was not so oppressive as our stereotypes often tell us. Family and community ties, religious practices, leisure pursuits—all were means of exercising autonomy and of easing an otherwise difficult existence. But there was no way to ease the harshness of life underground, in the mines themselves, and it would be hard to overstate the perils men faced when they were there. Here, our stereotypes hold all too true. Coal mining was indeed a dangerous and physically draining occupation. Tens of thousands of men were killed or maimed digging coal in southern Colorado. Even if a miner was fortunate enough to retire without ever experiencing a crippling accident, he was likely permanently hunched or had chronic back problems from working in underground rooms that were sometimes less than four feet high. And it was inevitable for a miner to retire with lung damage. Debilitating toil and extreme danger were the two hallmarks of mining coal, and the miner was keenly aware of these realities. "We tried to take care of ourselves the best we could in the mine," says John Valdez. "We all figure we're going in alive but we don't know if we was going to come back alive."[4]

Death and injury came in a variety of forms in the coal mine. Explosions caused by suspended dust or pockets of methane gas were the most dramatic

accidents, capturing headlines and shattering communities. Dev-
astation, tension, and sorrow descended on a camp in the wake of such a
disaster. Note this *Denver Post* reporter's description of the scene following an underground explosion in the Number 2 mine at Sopris in 1922:

> A hundred silent men and women are gathered at the mouth of the manway,
> watching, wondering, and waiting. There is no wailing, no moaning.
> The time for that has passed. All that can be done now above ground is
> to wait—to wait for the bell which will signal that another body has been
> found and is being brought to the surface.[5]

If the scene above ground was somber, the scene below ground must have
been downright horrific. A confined explosion deep in the earth was usually extremely violent. Miners typically carried numbered brass tags for
identification purposes in the event their bodies might be unrecognizable in
the aftermath of such an accident.

Although explosions were especially dramatic, they were responsible
for fewer than half of Colorado's mine fatalities. Most deaths came in
smaller numbers, when one or two miners working a face were crushed or
buried by rock falls. Many other killers lurked the mine—runaway mine
cars, exposed electrical wires, heavy machinery, cages, shafts, and fires.[6]
Men died often and quietly. Their deaths were reported in local papers,
usually without fanfare. "Two Italian coal miners, Carlo Filleppo and
Ferdinando Gandino, were caught in the Engleville mine at 11 o'clock today by a fall of fine coal," read a typical item in the *Denver Times*. "Instead of digging them out at once, three miners near them ran for help and
by the time the bodies were reached both of them were dead from suffoca-
tion. No bones were broken. The victims were both unmarried. Their
parents live in Italy."[7]

Coal mining consistently had the highest severity rate of injuries of any
major industry in the United States. It usually had the highest frequency
rate as well. As late as the mid-1940s, 900 to 1,250 miners were dying
each year nationwide, and fifty times that number were suffering injuries.[8]
Few men could spend a substantial amount of time in a mine without being
seriously injured at some time in their careers, and many were scarred for
life. Beatrice Nogare's brother was a young man working in the Del Car-
bon mine when "the whole top came down on him. And we never expected him to live. He got a big lump on the back of his spine and the
doctors don't dare operate on him or it would kill him."[9] The "Hospital
Bulletin" section of *Camp and Plant* ran countless reports on the status of

injured miners. A typical one matter-of-factly told of "Alexander, Robert, of Walsen—Admitted to the hospital last October, leg amputated. He is now walking about the hospital on a peg leg....Zaporello, S., of Berwind, who was sent to the hospital December 2 with a crushed foot, is now hobbling about the hospital on crutches."[10]

Tragically, Colorado's coal mines consistently exceeded national averages for deaths and injuries. The table below presents the fatality rates for every thousand miners employed in Colorado; for comparison, national averages are also given. Colorado's high accident rate can be attributed to three factors. First, the dry climate, combined with the low moisture content of the region's coal, created high levels of suspended dust, facilitating explosions. Second, the region's geology was characterized by severe upheavals, which weakened the rock around the coal seams. Rock falls and slides were therefore more frequent than in the mines of the East or Midwest. Third, unionization came late to the West. Safety was a major concern of the United Mine Workers of America, and where the union had a foothold—as in certain parts of the East—safety conditions were significantly better.[11] As we have seen, the UMWA did not achieve a stable presence in Colorado until 1933.

NUMBER OF FATALITIES PER 1,000 MINERS EMPLOYED

|  | 1884–1912 | 1913–33 | 1934–40 |
| --- | --- | --- | --- |
| Colorado | 6.81 | 5.02 | 3.00 |
| National average | 3.12 | 2.96 | 2.24 |

The elevated danger in Colorado's mines was statistically apparent to state inspectors, operators, and miners by the turn of the century. The UMWA used safety as a major rallying point during the Great Strike of 1913–14, accusing mine owners of criminal negligence, disobedience of the law, improper management, and inadequate ventilation, which combined to kill almost three times as many men as the average for coal mining in the United States.[13]

The era of the Great Strike was, if not a turning point in mining safety, the period when legislators finally began to hold the operators accountable for deaths and injuries in the mine. Prior to this period, a miner or the surviving members of his family were powerless to seek compensation in the event of death or injury. If compensation was received, it was on the operators' own volition and usually amounted to no more than a few hundred dollars for burial or moving expenses. To be sure, management portrayed themselves as more magnanimous than that. According to a mining engineer who worked for the Wootton Land and Fuel Company, owner Colonel Owenby spared "no expense" for hurt miners or surviving family, and he "looked after their interests" as long as they stayed in the camp.[14] Jesse Welborn, president of CF&I during this period, testified that the company paid an average of $1,000 to each of the families of the miners killed in the Starkville explosion of 1910. However, actual amounts depended on the size of the family.[15]

In any case, camp residents do not recall the operators being particularly altruistic. Compensation was doled out meagerly, if at all. Human life seemed a relatively low priority for the company. "Human beings didn't mean anything," says Don Mitchell. "[A runaway coal car would] come down like a streak of lightning. Super come down and he said, 'Hey, any mules killed?' That's the first thing he asked....Mule used to cost $250, and a man, all we'd do is hire another one. That's about the way they thought then."[16]

Angela Tonso recalls that even though miners would get medical attention, they would not receive any income while convalescing. "In them days if you get hurt...they put you in the hospital...," Tonso explains, "but you don't get no compensation. You didn't have no income. If you got killed in the mine, that was it. There was no benefit. If you save a dollar when you was working, OK; if you don't you was out. You was broke. And you have to depend on charity or good samaritans."[17]

According to miner Thomas Ward, the operators could be heartless when it came to caring for an injured worker and his family. A miner Ward knew broke his back and crushed his ribs while on the job. He laid in his galvanized two-room tin shack for three days before the company doctor came. The doctor sent the miner to the hospital, and the superintendent immediately came by and told the injured man's wife that, in Ward's words, "if she couldn't pay her rent she could take in boarders so she could get enough money to pay the rent." The following morning, "a Mexican came up there with a little spring wagon and loaded her furniture up and took it away, and she left the camp."[18]

Before 1914, three common-law concepts protected the mine operators from having to compensate their employees for injury or death. The first, the concept of "assumption of risk," simply held that when a worker accepted a job, he or she also accepted all the risks inherent in the work. The second was the "fellow servant" rule. Akin to "assumption of risk," this doctrine dictated that a worker who took a job also accepted the risks posed by careless fellow workers. This rule effectively meant that the operators were not responsible for any accidents in which language or ethnic barriers between miners had played a role. But a third common-law concept, known as "contributory negligence," was the most devastating of all to miners and their families, because it basically guaranteed that the operators would not be held liable for any accidents at all. In the words of historian James Whiteside, "contributory negligence" meant that "an injured worker, or his survivors, had to prove not only negligence on the part of an operator, but also that there had been no negligence whatsoever on the worker's part in causing the accident." It was virtually impossible for a miner or his survivors to meet such a burden of proof in the aftermath of explosions, fires, or rock falls—disasters that typically destroyed the evidence of their own causes.[19]

Not only were the operators protected by these prevailing concepts of common law, but also they usually had the political muscle to control the coroner's juries that convened to investigate mine accidents. In 1915, Huerfano County undersheriff John McQuarrie testified before the federal Commission on Industrial Relations about the bias that was built into coroner's juries. "I was always instructed," said McQuarrie, "when being called to a mine to investigate an accident, to take the coroner, proceed to the mine, go to the superintendent, and find out who he wanted on the jury. That is the method that is employed in selecting a jury at any of the mines in Huerfano county."[20] This method of jury-stacking was ruthlessly effective; not one personal-injury suit was brought against mine operators in Huerfano County between 1895 and 1915. Similar jury-rigging techniques were used in Las Animas County. When the Primero mine exploded in 1910, killing seventy-five men, the corner's jury needed only five days to decide that the cause of the explosion was unknown, thus shielding CF&I from any blame under the concept of contributory negligence.[21]

But the tide began to turn somewhat in that disastrous year. In 1910 alone, separate explosions at CF&I's Primero and Starkville mines and Victor-American's Delagua mine killed 210 men. The carnage prompted a horrified state legislature to make the first changes in the compensation laws.[22] The legislature repealed all "fellow servant" rules and replaced them with a statute that held employers responsible for injuries caused by coworkers. In theory this was a step forward, but the law also limited the damages to $5,000, and even then a well packed coroner's jury could still shield the company.  In 1914, more substantial progress was made when Colorado voters approved a measure abolishing the assumption-of-risk defense in cases when accidents resulted from "defective machinery, tools, or plant facilities that the employer should have corrected through ordinary diligence."[23]

Many miners associate the Great Strike of 1913–14 with the changes in the compensation laws, and indeed the widespread revulsion that followed the Ludlow Massacre may well have played a part in strengthening the miners' hand.  Don Bonacci, who broke his back in five places when the roof let go in the underground room where he was working, remembers that "that strike and the regulations" forced the operators to improve working conditions and compensate injured miners.  Bonacci received $3,600 dollars after his accident in 1936, money that allowed him to open a bar and restaurant in Walsenburg and earn a new living.  Compensation also helped Opal Furphy, a miner's widow, to survive after her husband, a rope rider in the Big Four mine, was killed by a runaway coal car.  "I had all four children" at the time of her husband's death, Furphy remembers.  "They were 12, 15, 18, 21.  They were all still at home.  My oldest son didn't marry until he was 29.  With compensation and [the oldest son's] help we made it."[24]

Although the compensation laws passed in the aftermath of the Great Strike offered some help to injured miners and widows, effective safety laws were still three decades—and thousands of deaths and injuries—away.  Not until the 1940s did Congress pass the Federal Coal Mine Inspection Law and the Federal Mine Safety Code, paving the way for stricter state codes.  By the late 1950s, fatalities in Colorado mines had dropped to 2.05 per 1,000 miners, just slightly above the national average.[25]

Miners worked ten to twelve hours a day, six days a week, with the threat of death or injury ever present.  Today, with our more advanced safety laws and employee-assistance services, it is difficult for us to conceive of the perennial stress the miner and his family faced.  Attempting to scratch out a subsistence income for himself and his dependents, a coal miner daily confronted the prospect of being crushed, burned, or blown apart.  And outside of his immediate community of friends and family, no formal mechanisms existed to help the miner or his family cope.

It is probably little wonder, then, that many turned to alcohol as an escape.  Liquor was a necessary part of a miner's life.  Not only did alcohol offer a way to deal with the stress of mining, but also the consumption of alcohol was an integral element of many immigrant cultures.  Drinking was also seen as an important masculine activity, as saloons provided places for men to go to socialize, commiserate, and escape the additional pressures of the home. So important was drinking to the miners' daily lives, testified CF&I president Jesse Welborn, that management "found that it is almost impossible to keep a force of men at the mines, unless they have that privilege [of drinking]."[26]  Similarly, Victor-American's John Osgood reported that saloons "seem to us to be a necessity of camp life."[27]

Welborn and Osgood must have come to such conclusions reluctantly, for liquor was in many ways the bane of the operators. It affected productivity, inflamed emotions, and made a largely disgruntled work force even more unpredictable. In periods of labor unrest, liquor, the operators believed, made the miners more susceptible to the appeals of union organizers and helped provoke strikes.[28]  But the proper way to control liquor consumption in the camps forever eluded the operators. "Saloons and drinking never cease to be a problem for the sociological worker," wrote Dr. Richard Corwin, head of CF&I's sociology and medical programs, in a 1901 report  "How best they may be disposed of or managed we do not feel sure." Efforts to mitigate the effects of alcohol consumption, for instance by operating company-owned saloons that prohibited the custom of "treating," an important part of many immigrants' drinking cultures, had worked to some degree, but "still there is room for improvement," admitted Corwin. He noted that outright prohibition of alcohol had only resulted in "blind pigs and wet bread wagons," which were even harder for CF&I to control.[29]

Whether administered by the company or by private businessmen, saloons were readily accessible to miners in virtually all of southern Colorado's coal camps. Primero, for example, had no bars on company property, but a number of privately owned saloons flourished just outside of town. In Valdez and other camps, CF&I leased company-owned buildings to private saloon operators, but the company kept a close watch on the way these establishments were run and could terminate the lease agreements at will.[30] Victor-American owned and operated saloons in its camps, but strictly regulated the hours of operation and prohibited the "selling of liquor to men who are already intoxicated."[31]  In the American Smelting Company's camp at Cokedale, the saloon—the Snake—stayed open until ten o'clock at night if work was scheduled for the following day, but "they went all night" when the mine was closed.[32]

CF&I's Sociological Department saw saloons as "poor men's clubs" but recognized that they served as a camp's social focal point. So the company tried to create alternative gathering places, such as reading rooms, recreational halls, and "soft-drink clubs" that took the focus off liquor. In closed camps, CF&I tried to modify the miners' drinking habits with a list of twelve rules that governed behavior in the "hard drink" clubs, such as the aforementioned "no treating rule," which prohibited patrons from buying drinks for others. Company saloons also tried to curb drinking by not extending credit to patrons.[33]

All the same, while the company sought to discourage excessive drinking, it had little choice but to tolerate those who imbibed anyway. Instead of being punished, drunks were usually just escorted home. The company did, however, take decisive disciplinary action if drinking became a problem. For instance, liquor-induced violence could get a miner expelled from camp, and it marked him with a lasting stigma that followed him to other camps.[34]

The operators kept the company saloons under tight control for a good reason: hard-working, hard-drinking miners tended toward rowdiness. Liquor was also a catalyst that could inflame Old World ethnic tensions. Irma Menghini's father operated a bar outside the Tioga camp in Huerfano County, and her memories reflect the ethnic squabbles that so often broke out. "A lot of Greeks were in the camp, and they were sort of a mean group of men," says Menghini, whose own family had come from Italy. "They fought a lot....My dad kept a gun, but he always hit men with the butt, he never fired it."[35] Even *Camp and Plant* would occasionally report on violence in the camp saloons. One particularly nasty scuffle occurred at a Starkville bar: "At 8:30 o'clock Sunday night of last week several Italians got into a row at Congvalli's saloon. One man was shot in the groin, while another was badly cut."[36]

Frank Wojtylka, who grew up in Cokedale, remembers the local saloon as a very intimidating place. His father would regularly send him to the bar for a bucket of beer, and "I was scared all the time when I was down there," admits Wojtylka. "You'd find a lot of guys at the saloon there, they'd be all over the porch stretched out drunk, with one laying here and then there's one laying there. You know, it'd be kind of hard for a kid to go down there as young as I was."[37]

Although saloons were popular, drinking at home was the normal routine for a miner working long days. The miner's lunch bucket, which was packed to the brim with fresh water and food early in the morning, conveniently served as a beer stein in the evening. Saloons charged ten cents to fill a bucket, and many miners would "go and get 10 cents" on the way home. Thirsty workers could buy kegs from the saloons as well, getting about sixteen gallons for three dollars.[38]   Many mining families also made liquor, wine, or beer in their own homes, a tradition carried over from Europe. "Everybody made wine," says John Tomsic. "They used to ship [grapes] in box car loads....All of the Italian people, the Greek people, and all of them."[39]   Alex Bisulco's family owned a produce store in Aguilar and stocked the ingredients for home brewing. They had, according to Bisulco, "a lot of grain and fruit and raisins and all that kind of stuff...And they had these big vats...and copper stills and that white mule would come out....It was 180 proof sometimes....It just had a kick like a mule in it, that's all. It was plenty strong."[40]

Especially after Colorado enacted prohibition, moonshining spread like wildfire through Las Animas and Huerfano counties.   "Most everybody that could made their own whiskey," remembers Albert Micek.[41]   Making whiskey—or beer or wine—was as popular as growing vegetables. During prohibition in Walsenburg, "everybody on 7th Street makes [booze] to help them make a living," recalls Louis Guigli. "And every once in a while...the federal man would come up and take samples of this wine and fine them $25 or $30 and leave them alone til the following year."[42]   There were "big whiskey operations all over [Huerfano] county," remembers Micek, and many—miners, townsfolk, and law-enforcers alike—profited from prohibition.[43]   As for the availability of liquor during this period, miner Gerardo Tovar chuckles, "Oh shucks, my, you know a lot of them cops got rich."[44]

Liquor not only helped miners cope with the stresses and dangers of mining, it also helped them cope with the inconsistent nature of the work. The ebb and flow in the demand for coal, both locally and nationwide, left the mines and their workers in a chronic state of instability. Statistics from a 1901 U.S. Industrial Commission report indicated just how unstable coal mining could be. A study of one Illinois mine showed that 210 men worked during one calendar year, but only 45 worked continuously. An analysis of that company's overall payroll showed that only 23 percent of the firm's 685 laborers worked constantly during the year. Between 1886 and 1899, bituminous mines nationwide operated just 171 to 234 days per year on average, equaling just 57 to 78 percent of full-time employment. The Industrial Commission report concluded that "This irregularity of employment naturally causes instability...[on the] part of the miners. To a large extent they are a floating population. They pass from one mine to another."[45]

Coal was mined in southern Colorado primarily for two reasons: to feed the great Minnequa Steel Works in Pueblo and to heat homes and buildings throughout the region during the winter months. Although a general boom lasted from 1890 to 1920, the pace of production at the Pueblo mill was susceptible to many influences, including overproduction, competition from mills in the East, and nationwide recessions and depressions. Mines supplying the mill could be shut down at a moment's notice. Seasonal fluctuations were more predictable, and most subbituminous and lignite mines, like those around Walsenburg, maintained skeleton crews during the summer months when little or no demand existed for domestic heating coal. Miner John Valdez, who worked in the Ojo mine ten miles west of Walsenburg, remembers the routine that played out each year when the weather turned warm. "The single guys used to get laid off in the summertime," he says. "They kept the married men, especially the ones living in the coal camps, in the company houses." Valdez himself was one of those who would be idled, but, he explains, "I use to feel all right about it because I didn't have no responsibility. I'd get up on a freight car and go look for something."[46]

The lack of work in the summer months could be a source of economic hardship, especially for those miners with large families, for whom survival was not as simple as catching a freight car. Some sought work in the fields during the harvest; others took on boarders. One study conducted in 1925 showed that in more than one-third of all coal-mining families nationwide, wives, sons, and daughters worked to supplement the family income.[47] Often this additional income made the difference between survival and destitution. In many respects the family was a single economic unit in which all members contributed to its survival. One Colorado miner explained a typical family income-earning arrangement: "We only stay during a portion of the year...[and] our wives do a little washing or something of the kind and earn small sums....We feel compelled to put our children to work...as soon as they are old enough to earn a dollar."[48]

Many mining families depended on credit from the company store to survive the summers, often putting themselves deep in debt by the time work resumed. Al Berte recalls that miners had "to work all winter to pay the grocery bill, because come summertime they had to charge all their groceries...for the whole summer."[49] Dan Desantis describes a similar scenario. "You used to go in debt in the summer...[and] over the winter whatever you make, you pay them," he says. "Sometimes you can't even pay the bill you made in summer. And you was in debt all the time."[50]

Widespread mobility was another result of these seasonal and economic slowdowns in the coal mines. Mobility was also a function of the general labor shortage during sustained boom times. Miners sought the best possible working and living conditions for themselves and their families. Moving from one mine to another was especially common among single miners, but evidence indicates that miners with families were prone to frequent moves as well. CF&I was instrumental in getting the state to standardize grade-school curricula so that miners' children who moved from camp to camp would experience minimal disruption in their education.

The experience of miner Thomas Ward was typical. Ward worked in Las Animas County for eight years between 1906 and 1914, and during that period he found employment at Wootton, Morley, Starkville, Bowen, Jewell, Aguilar, Green Cañon, and Frederick. Similar stories are legion. John Marzer, although only twenty-seven years old, had already mined coal in Sopris, Hastings, Berwind, and Starkville in Las Animas County and in Blosburg, Gardener, and Van Houten in New Mexico.[51] John Tompkins, in more than twenty years as a miner between 1920 and 1940, worked dozens of mines without ever leaving Huerfano County. "I worked the Black Hill Mine," Tompkins remembers,

> and then I worked at Big Four. Then I worked at old Turner. I worked at Little Turner. Then I worked at Maitland....Then I worked at all these others, worked at Barber and Alamo. And then I came up here and worked at Ojo. I worked at Ojo quite a while and then I went to Oakview....So I worked all around. I mined coal in pretty near every mine from Walsenburg up to, around and back up to Ojo.[52]

Stories like these cast doubt on the familiar contention that miners were held captive by their debts to the company store. In the coalfields of southern Colorado, at least, mobility, not captivity, was the miners' norm. Such mobility was a sign of both economic hardship and a highly competitive market for labor. As historian Crandall Shifflett points out, this mobility was common to all coal-mining regions. Shifflett notes a 1923 study in which the U.S. Coal Commission tracked miners in the bituminous fields. According to Shifflett, the study found such extreme mobility among the coal-mining population "that it was difficult to locate families in 1923 whose earnings and expenditures could be checked against a single mine-company payroll for an entire year."[53]

One crucial part of the mining communities that helped mitigate migrant miners' sense of dislocation were the ubiquitous ethnic lodges and societies. These organizations met a number of important needs. They brought together miners, usually of the same nationality, to share common experiences, grievances, and concerns. They functioned much like large extended families, so that new members of a camp could find a sense of belonging almost immediately by joining a lodge. The societies were "legal" in the sense that most operated in the open under a charter; although employees kept a suspicious eye on the societies' activities during periods of labor unrest, they typically did not blacklist or fire men belonging to these societies. Miners could thus freely band together in the lodges. All told, these organizations filled many of the same associational needs that a strong union—had one existed—might otherwise have provided.

Many societies existed in Las Animas and Huerfano counties, and their names reveal their strong ethnic basis. Italians had the Dante Alighieri Society, Nueva Italia, Pietro Toselli, and the Legabuchase or League Abrusi, to name a few. Austro-Hungarians had as many lodges as the once-great empire had nationalities, including the Slovenes' Narodska Protura, the Serbian-Montenegrin St. Peters Society, the ZMP, and the Croatian Fraternal Union. "Mainstream" fraternal organizations whose local lodges often took on ethnic characters included the Odd Fellows, the Knights of Pythias, the Moose, the Masons, and the Knights of Columbus.

To immigrants struggling to adjust to a new land, the ethnic societies represented a little piece of home. Miner Ed Tomsic, a Slovene, "started getting interested in the lodges right away" after he arrived in the coalfields. Lodges were especially valuable to newcomers like Tomsic because they sponsored many social activities, ranging from dances to picnics, traditional festivals to religious celebrations. Italian societies, for example, usually organized a large celebration for Columbus Day and another for St. John's Day, which fell close to the Fourth of July. Slovene lodges sponsored dances, "mostly the polkas," recalls Ann Laney, because the Slovenes were "noted for their polkas." Occasionally, several different lodges would band together to sponsor large events. In this way, ethnic societies served as a glue that held not just individual ethnic groups, but also entire multiethnic communities, together.[54]

A crucial function of the so-called mutual-benefit or mutual-aid societies, in particular, was to provide insurance to their members. Even after workmen's compensation laws began to operate in the miners' favor, mutual-aid societies were still needed to give widows and surviving families a sum of money—sometimes to help them return home, often simply to sustain them through the difficult economic period that inevitably followed the death or injury of a family breadwinner. In fact, providing financial support to bereaved families was the primary function of many a lodge. One member described the League Abrusi in Trinidad as "a couple hundred guys, and then somebody die. We'd pitch in a dollar apiece. Somebody get hurt, they get compensation from the lodge."[55] Insurance was also the main driver of the Dante Alighieri Society; "other than that," according to Irma Menghini, "they didn't mix in with politics or mix with strikes or anything like that."[56] Miner Rodas Mediniza, a member of the Serbian-Montenegrin St. Peters Society, testified to the activities of his eighty-two-man lodge: "The object of our society is the support for one another, helping one another out in sickness, taking care of the widows and children of the brothers, paying certain sums to the sick."[57]

Though miners and camp residents usually insisted that their societies were apolitical, lodges also offered a ready-made, tightly knit organization that fostered solidarity during periods of labor unrest. Many of the societies' charters prohibited members from working in strike zones. Ostensibly, such rules were simply meant to protect members from harm, but in many instances, those society bylaws were really a guise for discouraging strike-breaking.[58] And the rules were highly effective in guaranteeing labor solidarity; very few society members broke ranks with strikers. One miner was asked by a congressional committee whether members who violated the rule and went to work during a strike were actually expelled from the lodge. "I couldn't tell you," replied the miner, "because that never happened in our society."[59]

The operators seem to have been well aware of the union-like nature of many of these fraternal and ethnic organizations. During strikes or periods when labor-management relations were tense, the lodges were often prohibited from meeting on company property, the benevolence of their charters notwithstanding. When rumors of a strike circulated in March 1912—a full eighteen months before the Great Strike began—the operators quickly cracked down on suspicious groups believed to be a front for union activity. Four Victor-American company officials, revolvers drawn, broke up the weekly meeting of a Serbian society in Delagua. Twelve of the society's members were immediately discharged and kicked out of the camp. "We showed them our charter," one member would later testify, but "the superintendent said he did not believe in that charter."[60] Clearly, amidst a climate of rising tensions, the operators viewed the societies as potential troublemakers. Exactly what role the various ethnic organizations played during the Great Strike—whether they did indeed secretly collaborate with the union—is not clear, but the relationship between these societies and the United Mine Workers of America is a subject deserving of further study.

In the end, coal miners were incapable of distancing themselves very far from their work—the hours were simply too long and the dangers were too great. The men could not wash away the stresses of mining like they could the coal dust and dirt that stuck to their bodies at the end of a shift. Alcohol was a quick antidote; drinking helped mitigate the pain of the men's lives, served as a popular social activity, and helped maintain communal bonds. And the fraternal, mutual-aid, and other societies helped make up for the transience, instability, and dislocation that were such an inescapable part of everyday life. The saloons and lodges in particular posed a challenge to company control, but at the same time, they probably held the workers' discontent to a lower level than it might otherwise have been.

## Chapter Five

# A Woman's Life

*To the woman of American birth . . . fellowship with the American people is a powerful offset to . . . isolation, even though she may live in the remotest of coal-mining communities. . . . This is not the case with the woman belonging to the family of the foreign-born worker. . . . To her . . . the coal-mining community—whether populous independent town or isolated company-controlled mining camp—is America.*
—U.S. WOMEN'S BUREAU, 1925[1]

*But he don't touch nothing in the house. He don't care about kids if they were sick. They better be quiet in the night because he got to have his sleep. Yes sir. When he came just have his supper ready, yes sir....If he want to go honkey-tonkey someplace just let him go.*
—JOSEPHINE BAZANELLE, CAMP RESIDENT[2]

Probably no woman in the coalfields of southern Colorado ever saw the inside of a mine—tradition held that it was bad luck to allow women underground. And yet women in the coal-company camps were driven by the rhythms of mining coal just as surely as their husbands and fathers were. Miners were responsible for earning the wages that kept food on their families' tables and a roof overhead—but miners' wives were responsible for most everything else. Taken together, the wide-ranging responsibilities of women in the coal camps were often as physically demanding as digging coal itself.

A married woman living in a coal camp was expected to maintain her family, and especially the miner she had married. A healthy, well-fed miner worked hard and got paid; on this simple reality rested a family's tenuous stability. A wife not providing the required nourishment and care was thus seen to jeopardize family survival. She was the linchpin holding the household and the family together. A 1925 Department of Labor report concisely summarized a woman's importance to the coal-mining community. "Only the presence of the family can keep the mine worker in the mining region," explained the study, "and his wife therefore assumes an unusual importance in the basic industry. Moreover, the fact that the wife frequently looks after not only her own family but other mine workers boarding or lodging in her home gives her additional importance."[3]

The miner's working day began when he entered the mine and ended when he left it. In contrast, his wife's working day began when she rose—before him—and it did not end until she collapsed into bed eighteen or twenty hours later. A miner might find an hour or two to relax or socialize after a bath and dinner, but miners' wives enjoyed few such respites. In general, women in the camps worked far longer hours than men, and they had far fewer opportunities for social contact. The time of rest or recreation that came on Sunday must have seemed like an oasis amidst an endless desert of exhausting toil.

Marriage was often a practical arrangement in the coal communities. For a man, it offered stability over the desultory existence of boarding houses and bachelorhood. For a woman, it provided an escape from the social limbo of having to depend for survival exclusively on the family into which she was born. As such, an engagement often marked a woman's transition from childhood to adulthood. Although marriage could have a romantic element, the pragmatism of survival often drove the trip to the altar.

For eastern and southern European immigrants, the path to the altar could be tortuous. Many southern and eastern European men came to America already betrothed to women or girls from their hometowns. Once in the United States, they spent months or years stashing away small sums to pay for passage for their brides-to-be. One Tyrolean miner arrived in New York after World War I and worked his way to Walsenburg by way of Gary, Indiana. After three years he had saved enough money to bring his fiancé over, and they got married at the Catholic church in Walsenburg.[4] Many other camp residents had similar courtships.

As we saw in chapter 3, the immigration experience was often intimidating and frightening, especially for a young woman traveling alone. Arranging a reunion over thousands of miles often exacerbated the difficulty, as Johanna Micek's mother found out. After a thirty-day transatlantic voyage, the woman made her way by train to Walsenburg, where her husband-to-be was supposed to meet her. But, explains Micek, "The fellow that told my dad when she would get here must have told him the wrong day....My mother came a day earlier than what she was supposed to be here. When she gets to Walsenburg she gets off the train and nobody knows her language and she doesn't know anyone so she sits there."[5] After a waiting a day, Micek's mother was finally able to arrange a ride out to the Hezron mine, where she eventually found her fiancé. It was a nerve-racking ordeal for such a newly arrived immigrant.

Other immigrant women came to southern Colorado's coalfields without the security of having someone waiting for them. Often friends and relatives would coax them with stories of hundreds of eligible miners seeking wives. That these women traveled thousands of arduous miles to pursue such hazy prospects testifies to the bleak conditions that prevailed in much of Europe in the early twentieth century. Maria Batuello came over at the age of seventeen at the prodding of her aunt, who was already engaged to a miner in southern Colorado. Before leaving the Tyrol, Maria sent her uncle-to-be a picture of herself, which he showed to his best friend, who became interested in her. Maria and her aunt arrived in Walsenburg in March 1921, and after eight months, Maria was married to her uncle's friend by Father Liciotti in St. Mary's Church. Decades later, Batuello proudly displays the original picture she sent to her uncle: "This is me. I sent this here. This is what my husband fall in love with."[6]

Another woman named Mrs. Kakalecik came to her marriage through similar happenstance. "[She] came to this country to marry one man," explains her friend Opal Furphy, but "she had never met him before. He was living in the rooming house, and she didn't like the looks of the man she was supposed to marry." So when the rooming-house owner gave her the chance to pick out whichever man she liked, she chose Mr. Kakalecik instead of her original intended husband, and they were wed the following day. The original fiancé had paid the woman's way to America, so Mr. Kakalecik "had to pay the first man the money back."[7]

Many couples who had met in the old country tied the knot in the small churches of Huerfano and Las Animas counties. Others found marriage prospects only after they arrived. As for the immigrants' children—the second generation—they courted much like young people did in small towns everywhere in America, the difference being that romance budded in the gritty setting of a coal-mining town. John and Caroline Tomsic got married when they were eighteen and sixteen years old, respectively. Their simple courtship took place through camp functions such as picnics and dances: "They had a big dance hall in Berwind," remembers Caroline Tomsic. "That was the extent to our going out and having a good time."[8] Many couples were brought together by way of Saturday night camp dances. Another courting ritual was the "box social," in which the girls would prepare box lunches and lay them out on a table. A boy would pick a box and would then have lunch with the girl who had prepared it. "Sometimes it was a real fancy box...[and] sometimes it was real fancy girl," remarks Albert Micek, "and sometimes it wasn't."[9]

Courting was governed by the rigid folkways immigrants had brought with them from Europe. Marriage had acute pragmatic and economic implications, so courting was not to be taken lightly. Women in particular could ill afford to tarnish their reputations and risk reducing their chances of finding husbands. Louis Guigli grew up in the camps and remembers that his sister had only one suitor. "In those days there was nobody who could come to the house and pick up my sister. Because if they ever picked up my sister, that man was going to marry her," Guigli says. "So my sister was 15 years old and Frank Corrioso came to see my mother. And my mother says 'well, all right, you take her out, but be sure you marry her.' And sure enough he did."[10]

With the high frequency of mining accidents and natural calamities such as influenza epidemics, numerous widows and widowers could usually be found in the vicinity of the coal camps. A widow with children typically had to remarry as soon as possible—economic survival depended on it. Likewise, a widowed miner, especially one with children, had an immediate need for a new wife to run his household. Bill Massarotti's bittersweet description of his second courtship reflects the stark, practical side of a marriage. A friend of Bill's who owed him money on an accordion set him up with a new widow quite suddenly one afternoon:

> And we got to the house....She was available. And two kids. A boy and a girl. The boy was about 2 years old and the girl was about 4 or 5. This guy...he said "you're looking to get married, no?" I told him "who in the hell told you I was looking to get married." He said, "I know...why don't you ask her?" I start talking to her. Went on the porch, start going to her. And she said, "You're doing pretty good." I said, "How about getting married?" She said, "Sure....I am sick and tired of working on this farm." After one month we got married.[11]

Marriage ceremonies in the camps were simple affairs, with services often taking place in a local church in either Trinidad or Walsenburg. Many were married in the camps themselves in whatever structure served as the house of worship. Miner Clarence Cordova, for example, was married in the kindergarten building at Rouse. Receptions, modest by today's standards, were usually held in the home of a close friend or relative, with guests bringing food and providing music.[12] Ed Tomsic remembers weddings in Primero being extremely festive occasions, especially Slovene weddings, which could last up to three days. "Any time a Slovene get married," says Tomsic, "the mine don't work on the Monday cause they celebrate....Wine was in washtubs, not in bottles."[13]

For newlywed women, the excitement of the wedding ceremony soon faded, and life quickly settled into a daily routine of household chores and child-rearing. Women in the coal camps worked prodigiously to maintain their homes and families. Those families were often quite large by today's standards. In 1925, when the federal Women's Bureau compiled statistics for women in coal camps nationwide, it found that approximately 45 percent of coal camp wives maintained households of four to six people, and 25 percent cared for seven to eleven people.[14] For women to take care of such large families—along with the dwellings they lived in—was no small task. The women had to buy and prepare fresh food daily, and they had to tend the large garden plots many families used to supplement their diets. Women were also responsible for the full range of housekeeping chores—long before labor-saving devices, such as electric vacuums, refrigerators, dishwashers, and the like, were available. And the task of keeping the house clean was greatly complicated by the coal dust and dirt that constantly wafted through the camps and caked everyone and everything in black.

Women washed clothes manually with lye soap and a washboard, a tedious chore if ever there was one. But an even more backbreaking task was to haul the water for washing and other uses from the nearest well or streambed.[15] As late as the 1940s, a government report found that women were still hauling water over long distances. In many western mining communities, according to the report, "water haulage is left to tenants, who carry their supply for domestic use in milk cans, buckets, or other containers, frequently from distant sources."[16] After carrying and heating the water for her husband's daily bath, at least one woman even had to help him scrub off the dirt from the mine. "I had the tub full of hot water and he go down in the big tub and I had to scrub him down, front and back and dry him out and help him put on his socks and his shoes," remembers Josephine Bazanelle of her daily chore.[17]

Preparing meals was one of the most time-consuming of a woman's chores. The woman of the house typically had to prepare three meals from scratch every day, and often she was responsible for feeding all under her roof, including not just her family but also any boarders. Feeding a miner was enough of a challenge in itself. A miner used up enormous amounts of energy in his work—undercutting rock, boring holes for charges, laying track, timbering rooms, and loading thousands of pounds of coal into cars. The work was physically demanding, and the miner's body was a furnace that burned calories at a frantic pace. Necessarily, then, his diet was rich and hearty, and his appetite was voracious.

Meal-making responsibilities for the woman of the house began as soon as she awoke. She had to fix two meals right away: breakfast and lunch. Breakfasts were usually very large, consisting of eggs, meat, bread, and coffee. Along with this full meal, a wife also prepared her husband's lunch bucket. The bucket carried fresh water, along with all the nourishment the miner would get during his working day. Packing a full bucket was therefore something of a skill for the miner's wife. Usually she would fill the bottom half with water, often placing fruit in the water to conserve the dry space above. She would then fill the top half of the bucket with dairy products, meats, and carbohydrate-rich foods such as bread and tortillas. Quantity was all-important. "Well I'll tell you," remembers Caroline Tomsic, "when [her husband John] was young, you'd be surprised what kind of lunch I gave him. He had to have steak, he had to have sandwiches, pork chops, everything, slices of bread."[18] Josephine Bazanelle packed similar items into her husband's bucket, including sliced bread, cheese, salami, boiled eggs, even fried leg of cottontail.[19]

Mining-camp residents produced much of their food themselves, and not surprisingly the primary responsibility for maintaining the garden and the animals fell to the women. Camp residents shopped at the camp store for staples such as flour, sugar, and coffee, but they grew most of their own produce and hunted and fished for much of their meat. Almost every yard contained a large garden, which often yielded enough fruit, vegetables, and herbs to last through the winter. Ann Laney's family was typical; they would "can everything and save it for the winter months."[20]

Makeshift chicken coops and rabbit hutches were also popular. Frank Gutierrez remembers such animals playing a vital role in his diet: "The only thing that was an advantage was that we could raise chickens, rabbits, cows in the camp, anywhere you lived...and that was your next meal. You could depend on it."[21] And the country around the camps teemed with wild game, including squirrels, jackrabbits, birds, and fish. Such animals were very much in demand. One local youth caught carp in Martin Lake and sold them in the camps for twenty-five cents for two pounds. He often made twenty-five dollars a day.[22] Angela Tonso remembers that when her family caught fish, "that was a feast. That was a treat just like Christ-

mas."[23]   In the open camps, local peddlers sold a variety of fresh vegetables, fruits, and dairy products, and with the many ranches in Huerfano
and Las Animas counties, families could buy goat meat or mutton when a
little extra money was available.

In all the oral histories that discuss the miner's diet, one point is made
repeatedly:  food was not wasted.  Angela Tonso remembers that life on
poverty's edge compelled families to be thrifty:

> We used to buy ranch butter, you know, we bought it for 15 cents a
> pound.  And we used to get a pail of lard....The butter we used sparsely
> for the toast, sometimes not even that...because [we had only] one pound
> a month for the whole family.  But we used to use the lard instead, you
> know.  And when we fry something, you know, we saved that..., espe-
> cially a pork chop.  Oh, my God, that was a luxury then.  And we saved
> that grease, you know, pork chop grease to use it and use it.[24]

All told, women in the camps faced work that was all-consuming and
that left them with little time for much else.  Josephine Bazanelle describes
an ordinary day for such women.  "Everyone they tend their own business.
Everyone to their own house and by the time they are ready to lay down
and go to sleep they had no interest to do anything else."  Her own time,
she adds, was taken up largely by the never-ending task of making and
mending clothes.  "By the time you wash and iron and patching....Even the
stocking you mend it and mend and mend.  The pants, one patch on top of
the other....I used to make all the dresses for my two girls...so you don't
have no time.  You're just layed out when it was time to go to sleep.  And
you got up at 5:00."[25]

What is more, because the functions of the household never ceased,
women often had to work even when they were incapacitated.  Bazanelle
recalls having to labor even harder in the last days of her pregnancy.  "When
the time came [to give birth], well, they say, the time is ripe now," she
recalls of those days.  "[So] I used to bake bread, a big batch of bread and
wash all the clothes, iron all the clothes, be ready, because I say, well for a
couple of days [while giving birth] I have to stay put."[26]

Clearly, maintaining homes and families represented a major responsibility, and it entailed an exhausting, seemingly endless set of tasks.  Yet
these labors were not all the work the coal-camp women had to do.  In
many cases, women also had to engage in additional, income-earning work
in order to supplement the family income.  Such additional work became
especially crucial in times of mine shutdowns or layoffs that eliminated

men's income—episodes that were not infrequent, given the inherent instability of the coal industry.[27]

The 1925 Women's Bureau report found a large percentage of coal-
camp women laboring for wages. According to the bureau, there were
about half a million women in U.S. coal camps who were fifteen or more
years old, and of these women, more than three-quarters were married.
Eighteen percent of the wives—almost one in five—were gainfully employed.
Among black, Italian, and eastern European married women, that number
rose to more than 25 percent who were income-earners. Taking on boarders was by far the most common kind of employment for coal-camp women,
with laundry and housecleaning also offering income-earning opportunities. Most of all, the bureau found that these women's incomes were crucial to their families' economic survival. Taking a sample of 1,578 coal-
camp families, the Women's Bureau found that an overwhelming majority
of the working women—90 percent—contributed all or part of their income to the household. In bituminous-coal regions, more than half of the
working daughters surveyed contributed all of the money they earned.[28]

These statistics reflected data from the entire nation, but they shed light
on the experience of the miner's wives in southern Colorado. For example,
Angela Tonso's husband worked in many mines in Las Animas and Huerfano
counties, but Angela herself always had boarders in her home. She charged
three dollars per week to feed her boarders and to do their wash.[29] Beatrice
Nogare took care of her father and brothers who worked the region's coal
mines, but she also took on six additional boarders, giving her at least nine
miners to look after. The already weighty burden of work fell even more
heavily on women like these. "[Some women] have 4 or 5 extra men to
make board...," remembers Josephine Bazanelle, and those women "wash
and iron and make a lunch bucket [for them] and all that everyday."[30]

Not only wives but also single daughters contributed income to the
family. The same Women's Bureau study from 1925 reported that 32 percent of the single women over the age of fifteen held jobs and contributed
all or part of their income to their parents' household. And again, women
in southern Colorado seem to have conformed to this nationwide pattern.
When she was only twelve years old, Emma Zanetell began doing wash for
coal-camp residents in Las Animas County. "I wash everyday from one
house to the other, on the washboard," she remembers. The income she
earned was crucial to her family, since her father was sickly and could only
work part-time.[31] Emma might even be considered fortunate; many of the
single women in the camps needed work but found few opportunities. Na-

tionwide, according to the Women's Bureau study, this lack of work had a disruptive effect on mining families. "The limited opportunities for employment for young women in the bituminous regions are responsible for the departure of many daughters...from the mining regions...," concluded the bureau, "and make for an earlier breaking up of the family circle than would be the case in a more normal community."[32]

The backbreaking nature of a woman's work is mentioned frequently in the oral-history record. Many interviewees speak of the camp women with a tone of reverence and respect for the toil they faced day after day, month after month, and year after year. Miner Alex Bisulco summed it up: "I don't see how those women raised a family and took care of everything....I don't see how they could not go bugs."[33]

Adding to the drudgery of women's lives was the almost complete lack of recreational outlets for them. Although camp women participated in the communal recreation activities described in chapter 3, they had no outlet that they could call their own—nothing that allowed them to escape, even momentarily, from the pressures of the home and family. According to the Women's Bureau, the problem was particularly bad in company towns. "Very few company-controlled mining communities...made provision for recreation suited to the women in the camp," noted the bureau, "whereas the majority of the independent communities provided such recreational facilities."[34] In all the available oral histories of the southern Colorado coal camps, there is only one mention of a club specifically for women: the "Happy-Go-Lucky Club" in Cokedale, which was a dancing and bridge organization.

For a woman to survive the harshness of her coal-camp life—the incessant toil, the lack of recreational respite, the precarious reliance on a husband or father whose life could be snuffed out indiscriminately—she had to have a certain toughness, strength, and resiliency. Men faced constant physical danger in the mines, but according to historian David Corbin, "women encountered a subtler kind of danger at greater psychological distance...the ever present danger of losing her main source of security, her husband." This shared sense of fear and danger, writes Corbin, reinforced a concomitant sense of "unity and openness" among coal-camp women.[35]

Most of the time, such individual resilience and collective unity remained inconspicuous if not hidden. Women went about their daily work, spiritually and materially supporting their husbands and families, helping other women in the community who were ill or incapacitated. But during periods of labor unrest, these underlying strengths came to the surface. Strikes brought the acute danger that husbands and fathers might be replaced in the mines, thus posing a direct assault on the survival of women and their families. Women responded to the threat by participating heavily—and often militantly—in strike activities.

The crisis of a strike altered accepted cultural norms. Communities banded together to face the common enemy—the company—and traditional gender roles gave way to the exigencies of the struggle. During strikes women were perceived as fighters, equal to men. In the words of writer Zeese Papanikolas, the women sat "beside their husbands, no longer excluded, a part of the great affairs of the world, relied upon, needed to win the strike."[36] In his biography of Louis Tikas, a key leader of the Great Strike, Papanikolas considers the motivations behind women's militant activism. "They were challenging not only their own pasts, and their cramped rituals," Papanikolas suggests, "but the very structure of the industrial world itself. In the sudden opportunities of the strike, in its chance for action and voice, these women had more, it may be, to win than their men."[37]

Many of the women, especially those who had lived in the coal region since childhood, were exposed to the violent excesses that often accompanied strikes. Emma Zanetell's father was a German immigrant and a staunch union man. She remembers that he was badly beaten during both the 1893 and the 1903 strikes. During the latter strike, the family's house was blown up by a crude dynamite bomb that someone hurled through the front window. Perhaps radicalized by such harrowing experiences, Emma married a pit boss in July 1913 and moved into a tent colony two months later when the Great Strike began.[38]

Women demonstrated their militance in incidents before the Great Strike. During the 1903 strike, for example, a crowd of women attacked a Mr. Hightower, who was supervising the demolition of company housing from which striking miners had been evicted.[39] But the bitter strike of 1913–14 may have elevated women's militance to a new level. In numerous incidents, women vented their rage toward the union's enemies. In Segundo, a group of women attacked a pro-company priest and "compelled him to seek safety in flight."[40] And at the Walsen camp, female picketers assaulted a track layer who had refused to join the union. "The infuriated women rolled him in the mud and kicked him," writes historian Priscilla Long. "His cries brought several mine guards who chased away all but one woman. She jumped on the track layer and beat him over the head with a heavy bucket, breaking his nose."[41]

During the ten-day guerrilla-style war that followed the Ludlow Massacre, Angela Tonso remembers being on the front lines, smuggling guns past militia checkpoints. "We put the rifle under our coat there," she explains, "and half in the boots and half under the arm, and have our arm free so the militia they see that we ain't got nothing." She and other women used dry creek beds for cover as they spirited ammunition and food to the men. "We couldn't walk on the ground because they kill us just like they was watching for men."[42]

Mary Harris "Mother" Jones, the legendary labor leader from Pennsylvania, spent much time in the coalfields of southern Colorado during the Great Strike. She was a strong role model for camp women, bravely facing jail time and numerous deportations from the region. A clever agitator, Mother Jones made the most of women's moral influence, employing both direct action and indirect persuasion. She knew that women could push the limits of direct action because they "had a certain immunity from the worst violence," writes Papanikolas.[43] So in early 1914, when camp women organized a parade in Trinidad to protest Mother Jones's latest incarceration, they correctly predicted that the authorities would spare them from the kind of brutality that was regularly inflicted on pro-union men. At other times, the women applied their moral influence indirectly, for instance by "shaming" their menfolk into taking direct action themselves. According to Papanikolas, "[Mother Jones told] the miners...that if they were too cowardly to stand up against the coal operators and the [company-hired] thugs there were enough women in the country to beat the hell out of them."[44]

Such Mother Jones rhetoric may have verged on exaggeration, but it was inspired by the accepted wisdom that women in the mining camps were tough, strong, and willing to fight for stability and dignity. The woman's place in the community—as homemaker, mother, and caregiver—was largely determined, perhaps imposed, by the era's prevailing societal and cultural norms. But in fulfilling these demanding and exhausting responsibilities, women developed a deep-rooted strength. When their well-being was jeopardized by the death or debilitation of a husband or by the upheaval of a strike, this inner strength—this survival instinct—inevitably surfaced. In this sense, the women certainly contributed to the essence of the community as much as their coal-digging husbands.

## Chapter Six
# A Child's Life

*I went to school at Rouse til I finished the eighth grade. That was all. There was no high school. Then my daddy put me down in the mine.*
—CLARENCE CORDOVA, COAL MINER AND CAMP RESIDENT[1]

Mining coal and the strict routine of maintaining a coal miner's house dominated the lives of men and women in the coal camps. And so, too, a child's life played out against the gray background of the mine. Children lived in households that were dominated by their fathers' daily march into the earth and their mothers' never-ending struggle to manage a home in a dusty, isolated community. Children, too, were victims of the accidents that killed or maimed their fathers; they too felt the omnipotence of the company, and they too endured the traumatic strikes that upended the coal-camp communities.

Children grew up fast in the camps. As soon as physically possible, they were put to work around the house, taking on chores of progressively greater responsibility as they grew up, and learning to juggle these chores with schoolwork. Some camp children went on to high school, but many others graduated from eighth grade straight into adulthood. Fourteen-year-old boys were no strangers to the mine; their sisters were often married and raising families before reaching the age of sixteen.

To be sure, many of those who grew up in the camps have pleasant memories of their early years. Children did have time for fun and recreation—certainly more time than their parents enjoyed. But children spent most of their time occupied with school and chores. And everywhere they looked around them—at their mothers and fathers, at their friends and neighbors—children saw people working hard. Hard work was an accepted part of any child's life. It was a necessary lesson for survival in a coal town.

Like their modern-day counterparts, children in southern Colorado's coal camps started school at age four or five. Formal education began with kindergarten and continued at least through the fifth grade, with many children completing the eighth grade.[2] Resident Don Mitchell remembers that families in the community took schooling very seriously. "We used to all hike to Hill School," he recalls. "Never miss a day, no matter how deep the snow....There was no such thing as missing a day of school, no matter what kind of weather."[3]

A remarkably well-organized grade-school system was in place in Las Animas and Huerfano counties at the turn of the century. Dr. Richard Corwin, the head of CF&I's Medical and Sociological departments, was the man primarily responsible for creating this solid educational system. Education was a major focus for the Sociological Department when it was founded in 1901, but Corwin and CF&I were committed to improving education well before then. The first corporate-sponsored kindergarten opened in 1891, and according to the company, "its success encouraged the opening of schools in other camps."[4]

Because the avuncular Corwin believed a child's education should begin as early as possible, the Sociological Department made kindergartens one of its top priorities. But CF&I's kindergartens did not just teach reading, writing, and arithmetic. In fact, one of their primary goals was to assimilate or "Americanize" the children of immigrants, to compensate for these children's supposedly poor rearing and incomplete social development. As the preface to the Sociological Department's first annual report reasoned:

> It is difficult to change the way and manners of adults; their habits have been formed and are not easily altered. With age comes indifference, a desire to be let alone and a loss of ambition; but not so is it with the young. Children are tractable, easily managed and molded, have no set ways to correct and recast; hence the importance of kindergarten.[5]

Corwin clearly saw kindergartens as a prime opportunity to mold children at an impressionable young age, to improve them before their "ways" were irrevocably "set." He just as clearly believed he had a mandate to teach good manners and habits—in other words, to step in where immigrant parents would otherwise fail. Through the kindergartens, Corwin wanted his department to begin shaping the next generation of miners and miners' wives. The goal was to instill in the children a much stronger and more uniform sense of "American" values than those held by their immigrant parents.

Assimilation to "American" norms was a general goal of the educational process, and it subtly underlay many school activities. But the activities were meant to be fun as well. In kindergarten, children played games and sang. Christmastime was particularly festive. Mothers were invited to school to attend concerts and to open gifts their children had made, and the company gave candy, fruit, and other gifts—dolls for girls, drums for boys—to the kindergartners.[6]

By 1904, kindergartens were efficiently operating in Sopris, Rouse, Starkville, Engleville, El Moro, Pictou, Walsen, Berwind, Tabasco, Primero, and Tercio. Grade-school education, from first through eighth grade, was administered by local school districts that were theoretically independent of the coal operators. But in practice, since more and more of the schools were established on company property and built with company funds, the districts worked hand-in-glove with CF&I. CF&I also took the lead in supplying textbooks, selecting teachers, and building schoolhouses for camp residents.[7] The school district certainly served the company's needs, but all the same, the Sociological Department could take credit for a remarkably well-run and well-organized school system in CF&I's camps.

Given the remoteness of many of the camps, CF&I often dominated local school boards. In some places, the board consisted of the camp superintendent and his managers. This tight mechanism of company control could become a source of friction in periods of labor-management strife. In 1914, for example, a Segundo grocer named Levo Pedri testified that he had been prohibited from entering the neighboring camp of Primero the day school board elections were held. The clear implication was that CF&I had rigged the voting process.[8] Eugene Gaddis, Corwin's successor at the helm of the Sociological Department, admitted that the company dictated the selection of teachers and readily obtained the dismissal of those to whom they objected.[9] Not all residents seemed to mind this arrangement. Clarence Cordova, for one, speaks fondly of the camp teachers. "They had some of the best teachers," he remembers. But he too understood that the camp superintendent had the ultimate say in matters of education. "You know who had the say so about the teachers?" Cordova asks. "It's the supers. The supers used to hire the teachers. They used to pick out the teachers. If they didn't like a teacher, she wouldn't be there long. They would fire her and get somebody else."[10]

Recognizing the high level of mobility among mining families, Corwin worked directly with the state superintendent to implement a uniform grade-school curriculum, encompassing reading, math, science, writing, and art. The standardized curriculum ensured that a student's education would not be greatly disrupted if he or she began the school year in one camp and finished in another.[11]  For example, during any given week of the school year, all fourth graders in all camp schools were studying the same material.

Even the camp schoolhouses were all designed similarly.  Each had four rooms, two upstairs and two on the ground floor, and two teachers responsible for all grades.  This arrangement represented an improvement over county schools, where a single teacher was responsible for all eight grades.[12]

During the golden age of CF&I's Sociological Department—roughly the first decade of the century—the company was dedicated to its educational program.  The Department demonstrated great flexibility in accommodating the varying educational needs of its numerous camps.  The twin camps of Berwind and Tabasco, for example, initially shared a schoolhouse that was located in Berwind, a mile from Tabasco.  But the distance proved inconvenient for Tabasco residents, so in 1902 the company constructed "a new four room building...on an elevated knoll...midway between the residence districts of the two camps."[13]  In the Purgatoire River valley, the residents of Valdez, Segundo, and Primero sent their children to a schoolhouse in Segundo.  When a child was killed crossing the railroad tracks between the camps, a second school was opened that allowed children to attend school without having to negotiate the dangerous crossing.[14]

Regardless of its assimilationist motivations, CF&I's schooling program was quite successful.  The educational infrastructure established at the beginning of the century served camp residents well into the 1940s.  Thousands of Las Animas and Huerfano county youngsters were educated in camp schools.  As early as 1914 the company could claim that the schools at Starkville and Sopris were graduating more students than any other two school districts in Las Animas County.  "Over 35 percent of all eighth grade graduates in Las Animas county have come from the CF and I company camp villages," boasted a company report that year.[15]

The schools in Huerfano and Las Animas counties reflected the diverse ethnic makeup of the population.  Martha Todd recalls that the camp schools and the high school in Walsenburg were true melting pots.  "I went to school right here in Huerfano County," she remembers, "I think with every nationality of child except oriental.  I don't remember ever seeing an oriental child."[16]  No one in Louis Guigli's family even spoke English until he and his siblings started going to school.  "Before we went to school the whole family only spoke Italian," he claims.[17]

Although the student body was multicultural for many generations, diversity could at times be a source of friction in the schools.  August Andreatta, the son of Italian immigrants, dated Hispana girls in school, which caused a number of scrapes with Hispano boys. "[They would] call me Dago," Andreatta says. "And Dago, see this didn't go [over well] with us, because Dagos are South Italians, way down in the boot. And us guys from way up there, high [in northern Italy], we didn't get along with the southerners. So, boy, we'd get to fighting."[18]

If they went to school in the larger towns, the sons and daughters of miners also faced prejudice against their families' social and occupational status. Don Mitchell, who went to school in Walsenburg, remembers that outside the camps mining families were stigmatized, and often the school-children bore the brunt of disdain. "Miner was rated nothing even by your businessmen in town," he explains. "I know when we went to school here, even in the schools we was treated different. Hell, I fought my way through schools here and I got to be quite a fighter from just [being a miner's son]."[19]

Only a small percentage of the students making it through the eighth grade went on to high school. For most mining families, it was simply too inconvenient and too expensive to send their children to high school. Beatrice Nogare's brother, for instance, graduated from eighth grade directly into the mine. "My parents did not have the money for him to continue his education," Nogare says. "He went to work in the mines instead."[20] Alfred Owens's family faced the same economic pressure; he could only make it through the fifth grade. "I had to go to work and help raise the family," he recalls.[21]

High school was expensive because none of the schoolhouses were located in the camps themselves. To attend, students had to arrange transportation to Trinidad or Walsenburg, or their families had to move closer to town, which then put the burden on the miner to commute out to the mine—a sacrifice few were willing to make. Also, the public high schools charged one dollar a month in tuition, which was often prohibitively expensive for mining families that were already financially strapped. August Andreatta had dreams of being a lawyer, and his teacher was willing to cover his high-school tuition in exchange for household chores. "She said: 'All you have to do is run my errands and bring me in coal and wood,'" Andreatta recalls. "She'd give me free board, and school. And I argued with my dad for two and a half months...[but] finally I had to give up. 'If that's the case,' [Andreatta's father] said, 'you got to help me raise the rest of the kids.' I ended up being a nobody. Nobody."[22]

Even if they could have afforded it, many miners simply did not believe that their children needed a high-school education. Such skepticism stemmed in part from the industry-driven environment of the coal camps, which favored practical skills over "book-learning," and in part from immigrants' old-country values, which often devalued and discouraged education for young women. Johanna Micek was quite familiar with the latter attitude. She was the first member of her family to graduate from high school, but while she was attending, her father continually badgered her to drop out. "I remember my dad saying, 'A girl doesn't have to go to school,'" Micek says. "He wanted me to quit school after I finished eighth grade because he said that girls didn't have to go to school. [He felt that] as long as she knows how to cook she doesn't need to know anything else."[23]

Many children succumbed to the pressure to quit school. Martha Todd began high school in Walsenburg with five other classmates from the Pictou camp; four years later, she was the only one to graduate. "At that time a good many of our girls were getting married very young," she says, explaining the high attrition rate. One of her friends started high school and quit to get married at the age of sixteen—"and she was the star student."[24]

For all the obstacles standing in the way of young women's education, young men seemed to face even greater pressure to forego school and begin earning wages, usually in the mine. Of the twenty-eight graduates of Walsenburg High School in 1923, fifteen were boys and thirteen were girls, and this was the first class to graduate more boys than girls. "I think that tells you a little bit about the times," says Martha Todd. "The boys went to work."[25]

Not all former camp residents look back and feel that they were robbed of an education. Many young men were in fact happy to quit school and begin earning a wage. Bob Tapia, who grew up in Cokedale, remembers that he and his friends were eager to get into the mine. "Boys wanted to go to work cuz most of them didn't want to go to school," he says. "I know that was my attitude. I didn't care anything about school. I quit when I was in the eighth grade. I was 14 years old and I didn't want no more school. So I asked the Super for a job....The first job I did was picking slate."[26]

A boy typically began work inside the mine at his father's side, helping to undercut the seam, clear the work area, prepare the charges, and load coal. Although Colorado had child-labor laws requiring a mine worker to be fourteen years of age, these regulations were widely ignored by employers and by parents. The American Smelting Company actually did require miners to be sixteen, but Frank Wojtylka circumvented the rule with his father's knowledge. "I went in digging coal with my dad. I was 15 so I told them I quit school, so I told the Super I was 16 and they finally let me go to work....But I lied about my age," Wojtylka recalls.[27] Economic necessity made parents unwilling to see child-labor laws enforced, and they often signed false affidavits claiming their boys were the minimum age to work.[28] The boys' youth was sometimes strikingly apparent. One fourteen-year-old, remembers Albert Micek, "wasn't very tall. He just dragged his coal mine bucket into the mine because he wasn't tall enough to hold it."[29]

Boys who went into the mines independently of their fathers began their careers with mundane tasks, such as picking slate out of the mined coal. Pete Baione got a job as a breaker boy at the age of ten. "I started picking slate," he says of his work. "You know they got big screens, shake the coal and pick all the rocks out."[30] Older boys could get work "trapping"—opening and closing large wooden shaft doors as the trips (the trains carrying coal or men) passed by. Although the job was mundane, it was crucial because proper ventilation of the mine depended on specific passages being blocked.

By the age of thirteen or fourteen, a boy might be given the responsibility of driving the mule trains that hauled coal and men around the mine. Alfred Owens graduated to mule driver at the age of sixteen after trapping for two years. Given the restricted space in the mine, the weight being hauled, and the number of animals in a team, he found it difficult and dangerous work. Don Mitchell's brother was only thirteen when he became a mule driver, "and he had a man's job. Drove a mule and that was a man's job."[31]

The danger that stalked the coal mines of southern Colorado had no regard for age. Boys died alongside their fathers in explosions, rock falls, and fires, and they often contracted respiratory ailments early in life. The mine was a rugged place, and boys who had barely entered puberty were forced to cope with the intense physical, mental, and emotional stresses of working in exhausting and dangerous conditions. Irma Menghini's future husband went into the mine at age thirteen and was seriously debilitated by the age of twenty. "Then he had to get out," says Irma. "He got pneumonia, broke an arm...and developed a sort of—not asthmatic...he couldn't breathe as well."[32] Alex Bisulco quit school in the seventh grade, and his friend Frank Regio got him a job as a trapper. A few months later Alex watched as Frank was killed by a runaway coal car. After five decades, Alex could still vividly recall the incident:

> We used to have to check the trips that came by with the motor....Because they used to lose cars back there. They'd bump together and come

loose and it was swampy....Frank Regio he jumped in the track to try to flag the motor down [because he was missing cars] and then two cars hit him, killed him too. We had to lift the cars off of him and everything. And after that I worked about 2 weeks, I couldn't take it anymore. I quit....I just couldn't work there no more, that's all.[33]

Sadly, Frank was actually the second person Alex had seen killed in the mine. A few weeks prior to that he had seen a man electrocuted. "He was all wet from sweat and his lamp touched that trolley line, killed him that quick, like that."[34]

Girls may not have faced the deadly horrors that their young brothers too often experienced in the mines, but they too lived lives of hard work, far removed from the circumstances of more privileged American children. Young unmarried women worked long hours doing household chores, either assisting their mothers or running homes on their own. "The girls would help one another," remembers Alfred Owens. "My mother would get up and fix breakfast...and the girls would clean up the house and wash dishes. They [took] care of the inside and helped with the little children too."[35] In many cases, the need for a second or third girl to help maintain the home was as urgent as the need to get an able-bodied boy to start bringing home a paycheck. As a result, like the boys, few girls in the coal camps continued school beyond the eighth grade. Ann Laney's older sister assumed the role of woman of the house after their mother died of influenza. "She was older than I am," says Laney. "In fact they just kind of passed her through in the 7th and 8th grades, and she stayed at home. My dad wanted me to take one year of high school, and then have her go the other year, and then me a year, and she didn't want that, and so I went ahead and finished high school. So she stayed home and took care of the family and washing and everything."[36]

Not only mining families needed their daughters' help. Irma Menghini's father was a onetime coal miner who opened up a grocery store. He pulled Irma out of school when she was twelve to drive the delivery truck. "I drove a Model T, and went to all the camps, up as far as Alamo, took orders one day, delivered them the second day," remembers Irma. "The third day I would go south to those mining camps and take orders and deliver them."[37]

Although the majority of a child's life was occupied by school and chores, and soon after that by wage labor, camp children did have a fair amount of time left over for fun and games. Many who grew up in the camps would support Al Berte's contention that life for a youngster "was wonderful." The games and pastimes were far simpler back then, but no less enjoyable. "That was a good place to raise your children," Berte insists, "because we had plenty of wide open spaces there. I was brought up like a rough neck, you know. It was nothing for us to go down to the river and...dive and swim and everything. And everything we enjoyed out there was all home made stuff."[38]

The geography and climate of the southern Colorado foothills gave children an opportunity to enjoy many different outdoor activities in both summer and winter. During the summer, children would play such timeless games as kick-the-can, run-sheep-run, and of course baseball. Cards and board games like dominoes and Polly Angie were also popular.[39] The children in the camps often learned games from cultures other than their own. "There used to be a Mexican game they called shinney, and it's something like golf," recalls Alfred Owens. "It had like a golf stick. In fact we used to go up in the woods and get wood and bend it. You see it had a bend and you had a ball and you couldn't pick it up with your hands. You just hit it with the shinney and you'd go from goal to goal."[40]

In the winter, children would ice-skate and ride shovels in the snow. Not only were these games fun, but also they served to strengthen the sense of community. Albert Micek remembers the children would "ice skate and in the evening all the neighbor kids would come and build a bonfire and roast wienies and marshmallows and skate on the ice." The children created their own entertainment together, "cause at that time we, well, up to about that time we didn't even have a radio."[41]

CF&I, through its Sociological Department, tried to impose greater order on children's activities by founding boys' and girls' clubs in the camps. The clubs were governed by elected officers and met once a week. Members would play games, act out stories, and participate in dances, contests, gymnastics, military drills, and music. As with the educational curriculum, the company meant for these activities to "improve" the children. For instance, according to a CF&I report, "Dances and rhythm work were particularly emphasized to give these heavy children a more graceful carriage and freedom of movement."[42] Also like the schools, the clubs helped teach "American" values and "proper" gender roles. The girls' clubs were organized much like the boys', but with "sewing and other practical domestic work taking the place of boys' athletic and drill work."[43]

To justify the establishment of children's clubs, the Sociological Department adopted the same accusatory tone that it used to explain the need for kindergartens—that is, it suggested that working-class immigrants were incapable of adequately raising their own children. he 1901–1902 department report had this to say about the young sons of immigrant miners:

> The typical boy of the coal camps is an interesting personage....His horizon has necessarily been limited; his whole training and environment has cultivated in him a narrow spirit, a selfishness which fails to see any good in a movement which does not benefit him personally....It is his delight to hang around the saloons, listening to the ever present accordion, learning to drink—he is already a veteran tobacco user—and taking fascinating lessons in profane and vile language.[44]

Such statements amounted to a not-so-subtle indictment of the drinking culture and social habits of European immigrants. And it implied, once again, that the company had a mandate to enlighten the miners' sons, who might otherwise be influenced by that culture to live lives of moral deficiency.

The Sociological Department viewed mining-camp girls from the same oversimplified, myopic perspective. To be sure, the company did not paint quite as dire a picture of the girls as it did of the boys. "Not having been turned out on the streets to amuse and care for themselves," the CF&I report generalized, "the girls are more refined and subject to fewer temptations [than the boys], and their problems, therefore, are much easier to solve."[45] But the unmistakable implication was still there that the company saw fit to "solve" these immigrant girls' "problems." Perhaps not surprisingly, camp children seemed to have limited interest in participating in these paternalistic, company-sponsored clubs. They probably had plenty of other amusement to enjoy.

Children in the coal camps grew up fast, but not necessarily any faster than their counterparts in other laboring households of the period. The image of the child-miner is powerful and moving when viewed from our late-twentieth-century perspective. Today, we hold sacrosanct the idea that youngsters should be nonworking, shielded from danger or toil; few images are as disturbing as that of the suffering child, slogging dull-eyed and underfed through a miserable existence of hard labor. Many reformers of the time—and some labor historians of today—have difficulty avoiding this suffering-child image. It seems an especially strong indictment of the morality of capitalism. When we see that child in the pages of history, we *know* that the men of capital have the blackest of souls.

But the evidence from the southern Colorado coal camps does not fully support this disturbing version of a child's life. Children in the camps did what children do today: they went to school, they played, they did household chores. Granted, they were more likely to experience the trauma of industrial calamity, and their chores were especially arduous in the era before domestic appliances, but they were certainly not lifeless shells. The chief difference between childhood then and now is that children in the camps were forced to grow up much more quickly. Today, we can remain children well into our twenties and sometimes beyond. In the coal camps, one might be a child at ten, but an adult by fourteen.

*Chapter Seven*
# Conclusion

The demand for coal from southern Colorado's mines began to wane after World War I.  By the 1920s, petroleum derivatives had eclipsed coal as America's primary fuel.  To be sure, society's transition from coal to oil occurred gradually, and coal mining remained a significant part of southern Colorado's economy for some time.  The industry even saw a brief revival during World War II.  But the general decline resumed in the postwar era.  Mine after mine shut down in the late 1940s and throughout the next decade.  In 1954, Colorado produced a total of three million tons of coal, the lowest annual amount since 1889.[1]  The once-bustling towns of Trinidad and Walsenburg went into long-term hibernation, subsisting on the relatively meager returns from ranching and small-scale tourism.

The coal-company towns of Las Animas and Huerfano counties closed down in rapid succession throughout the 1930s and 1940s.  Along with the general decline in the demand for coal, the automobile played an important role in consigning the camps to obsolescence.  The widespread availability of cars meant that miners no longer had to live in immediate proximity to the mines; cars thus redefined the miners' relationship to the company, removing many of the contentious issues that had arisen from the operator's omnipotence within the company town.  The majority of the remaining miners chose to commute to work from Trinidad or Walsenburg, or from smaller but still independent towns like Aguilar, Weston, or Valdez.

Most of the coal camps were eventually razed or abandoned.  CF&I asked the last eleven residents of the Walsen camp to leave in 1965, then bulldozed everything but the camp's small power plant.  Today, the quick-eyed motorist can spot the plant's crumbling shell on the north side of Route 160 just west of Walsenburg.[2]  Sopris, one of the oldest and most productive coal towns in Las Animas County, now sits at the bottom of Trinidad Lake.  During World War I, Sopris had a population approaching 2,000.  But the mine shut down in 1940, and by 1970, when the Army Corps of Engineers finished the dam designed to save Trinidad from the springtime rampages of the Purgatoire River, only 300 residents remained.  They were forced to relocate as the reservoir began to fill.  "Because Sopris never bothered to incorporate," wrote an observer of the town's demise, "the government did not have to build new houses for the people or move them to a new location. They were simply paid a sum of money for their places and told to move, and their homes were bulldozed into piles of rubble."[3]

Residents of the American Smelting Company's town of Cokedale fared a bit better after the Boncarbo mine shut down in 1947. American Smelting sold the town to the Florence Machinery Company of Denver, which in turn put the houses up for sale, charging $100 per room and $50 per lot. Most of the town's seventy-two homes were sold, at $450 each, to the coal miners who had been tenants.[4] Cokedale's residents jumped on the historic-preservation bandwagon in the 1970s, restoring all of the town's coal-era structures, including the superintendent's house, the company store, the recreation hall, and the school (see figure 9). Today the town appears much as it did when coal was king—a little neater maybe, but essentially still a coal town at heart. The crumbling remains of the town's three hundred coke ovens still sit quietly just south of the town on the other side of Route 12.

The coal-company town has become obsolete in southern Colorado, and there is little physical evidence left to show us how miners and their families once lived. But one need only leaf through the Huerfano and Las Animas county telephone books to get a sense of the industry's legacy. The names of onetime immigrants are everywhere: Lenzini Motor Company, Zorc Home Improvement Center, Benfatti Furniture, Ludvik Propane and Gas, Hobeika Ready-to-Wear Clothes, Ferrero's Dozer Service, Maniscalco Brothers Wrecking Company, Salbato's Cabinet Shop, and Fred A. Menghini, D.D.S. Walsenburg and Trinidad absorbed many of the mining families after the company towns closed, and descendants of these families have become mayors, bankers, bartenders, merchants, schoolteachers, construction workers, doctors, lawyers, and car salesmen.

Life in the coal camps could be harsh and oppressive, but it was hardly the strife-torn existence or the utter enslavement some historians would have us believe. Trying to capture the essence of the mining family's experience by looking solely at cataclysmic labor conflicts is like trying to assess the 1950s by looking solely at the Korean War. Yes, to a large extent the miners were exploited by the operators, and great inequities and injustices existed in the form of poor safety conditions, the scrip system, the operation of the company store, and the operators' broad power over the lives of their laborers. But life in the camps was passable, especially when evaluated by the standards of the era. The oral histories are replete with the reminiscences of people who enjoyed camp life. Former residents look back fondly on the friendships they built and the strong sense of community they forged with their fellow townspeople. They remember the time they spent socializing, relaxing, playing baseball, going to dances, drinking home-made wine, attending school, hiking the Spanish Peaks, and fishing the Purgatoire.

The labor union was certainly an important part of a miner's life, yet it was hardly the focal point one might think. Undeniably, the UMWA played a significant role in politicizing and radicalizing miners, in educating immi-grants and providing them with valuable insights into the hierarchies of power in American society. But before 1933, the union appeared for only a few months every ten years or so. During the long periods in between, coal-camp residents struggled through life without any assistance or guid-ance from organized labor. It was the community, far more than the union, that provided moral and spiritual support to individual miners and their families.

Two characteristics distinguished the experiences of mining families from the experiences of their counterparts in other industries. The first was the extreme diversity of ethnicity. The multiethnic makeup of the camps stood out in sharp relief when compared to most other small towns of the day, and this diversity was heightened by the relative isolation of the communi-ties. Immigrants in the coal camps banded together with others like them-selves, just as immigrants did in towns and cities all across America. But in remote southern Colorado they may have banded a bit more tightly to cope with the harsher aspects of mine work and company-town life. Many resi-dents sought familiarity and comfort in ethnic subcommunities, maintain-ing the customs and lifestyles of their native culture. Some residents, in fact, were able to function for years without having to learn English. These conditions perpetuated a stronger sense of ethnicity than typically devel-oped in larger, less isolated, and more open towns.

The second characteristic that distinguished the camp dwellers' experi-ence was the extreme and inescapable danger of mining. Life and survival were constantly precarious for miners and their dependents. Mining acci-dents, fatal or otherwise, were almost daily occurrences. The stress associ-ated with this reality was intense, and it influenced every aspect of camp life. The dangers of mining brought the communities close together, and new families were quickly accepted into existing community structures. Mining families supported each other, often despite traditional ethnic ani-mosities, because the perennial stresses of the mining lifestyle were simply too difficult for anyone to face alone.

Ultimately, then, it is difficult—and probably inadvisable—to try to draw sweeping conclusions about life in the coal camps of southern Colorado. The reality was contradictory and complex. Hearing residents' reminiscences of close ethnic-group cohesion, or of the friendships that crossed ethnic lines, we might be tempted to romanticize the company towns as tightly knit communities, far superior to our fragmented and alienated "neighborhoods" of today. But to do so would be just as wrong as concluding that company-town life was grinding, draconian, relentlessly miserable. In fact, as we have seen—as we hear when we listen to the camp residents' voices—neighborly warmth coexisted with ethnic and racial animosity; danger and oppression cohabited with leisure and joyous self-expression. If life in the camps was often exhausting and dangerous, so it was at other times exhilarating and enjoyable—or depressing, funny, heartwrenching, playful, tedious, bittersweet.

In some ways the lives of coal-camp residents seem unfamiliar, even unfathomable to us. Today, few of us can imagine living our entire lives within a four- or five-mile radius, or using a fast-running stream and a bucket as a plumbing system. Many of us are lucky enough that we do not have to marry and raise children at the age of sixteen; we do not have to watch our friends die violent deaths before reaching adulthood—and we can hardly fathom what it must be like to do so.

But just as it would be a mistake to fixate on either the bright or the grim side of coal-camp life, so too would it be wrong to view the coal-mining families as completely unlike us. In fact, in many ways their aspirations were much like ours. Coal-camp residents may have lived spartan lives, carving out a modest existence through work so hard we can barely imagine it. But those camp-dwellers who survived the mines, the strikes, and the depressions often achieved a version of the American dream not so different from what many of us seek today. Many of them eventually bought small pieces of property and homes; many had enough left over to buy Chevys or Fords, or even to send their sons and daughters to college. We might say they were "Americanized," but we might just as well say that they helped, in their one small corner of Colorado, to shape what is "American." In the end, when we listen to the stories of the southern Colorado coal-camp residents—stories both shocking and mundane, told by people both unassuming and heroic—we glimpse a vital part of the American experience.

# Notes

## Chapter 1: Coalfields, Companies, and Unions

**1**
U.S. Department of Labor, Women's Bureau, *Home Environment and Employment Opportunities of Women in Coal-Mine Workers' Families*, Bulletin of the Women's Bureau, no. 45 (Washington: Government Printing Office, 1925), 11.

**2**
Crandall A. Shifflett, *Coal Towns: Life, Work, and Culture in Company Towns of Southern Appalachia, 1880–1960* (Knoxville: University of Tennessee Press, 1991), 27.

**3**
Ibid., 30.

**4**
Besides bituminous, coal comes in two other grades: anthracite and lignite. Anthracite is a very dense coal; it is difficult to ignite, but it burns cleanly, so it was used primarily as a domestic heating fuel in heavily populated areas of the East. The country's only major anthracite field lies in eastern Pennsylvania, although small seams were mined for years in Crested Butte, Colorado, and Madrid, New Mexico. Lignite is a softer coal that contains high amounts of organic matter. Colorado's northern field produced lignite, and this grade was used as a source of domestic fuel throughout the region.

**5**
H. Lee Scamehorn, *Pioneer Steelmaker in the West: The Colorado Fuel and Iron Company, 1872–1903* (Boulder, Colo.: Pruett Publishing Company, 1976), 15–18.

**6**
Ibid., 19, 40–46.

**7**
Ibid., 67–68.

**8**
Ibid., 82–90.

**9**
Ibid., 1–2.

**10**
Ibid., 119.

**11**
Ibid., 102–3.

**12**
Ibid., 124.

**13**
*Denver Times*, December 31, 1899, 23.

**14**
*Denver Times*, November 20, 1900, 11.

**15**
Scamehorn, *Pioneer Steelmaker*, 165–68.

**16**
Ibid., 126, 139.

**17**
In the southern field, these smaller operations included the Occidental Coal Mining Company, the Huerfano Valley Mining Company, the Trinidad Coal and Coke Company, and the Prospect Point Coal Company, to name just a few.

**18**
Donald J. McClurg, "Labor Organization in the Coal Mines of Colorado, 1878–1933" (Ph.D. diss., University of California, 1959), 39; Scamehorn, *Pioneer Steelmaker*, 61–63.

**19**
U.S., House, *Reports of the Industrial Commission on Immigration and on Education*, 57th Cong., 1st sess., 1901, H. Doc. 184, 407.

**20**
McClurg, "Labor Organization," 102.

**21**
Ibid., 127.

22
U.S., House, Committee on Mines and Mining, subcommittee, *Conditions in the Coal Mines of Colorado: Hearings before a Subcommittee of the Committee on Mines and Mining*, part 2, 63rd Cong., 2nd sess., 1914, 663–64.

23
Beatrice Nogare, interview (transcript), Huerfano County Ethno-History Documentation Project, Huerfano County Library, Walsenburg, Colorado (collection hereinafter referred to as "HCEDP".

24
Maria Batuello, interview (transcript), HCEDP.

25
McClurg, "Labor Organization," 197–98.

26
Ibid., 205–6.

27
George P. West, *Report on the Colorado Strike*, report prepared for the U.S. Commission on Industrial Relations (Chicago: Barnard and Miller, 1915), 6.

28
McClurg, "Labor Organization," 380.

29
Ibid., 355.

30
Ibid., 347.

31
James Whiteside, *Regulating Danger: The Struggle for Mine Safety in the Rocky Mountain Coal Industry* (Lincoln: University of Nebraska Press, 1990), 124–25; McClurg, "Labor Organization," 349.

32
Beatrice Nogare, interview (transcript), HCEDP.

33
Don Mitchell, interview (transcript), HCEDP.

34
Donald Mitchell, interview (transcript), University of Colorado, Institute of Behavioral Science, Coal Project, Norlin Library, Western Historical Collections, Boulder, Colorado (collection hereinafter referred to as "UCCP").

35
McClurg, "Labor Organization," 429.

36
Whiteside, *Regulating Danger*, 29; McClurg, "Labor Organization," 387.

37
McClurg, "Labor Organization," 434–35.

38
Ibid., 446–54.

39
Ibid., 456.

40
Ibid., 513.

41
Ibid., 533.

42
Donald Mitchell, interview (transcript), UCCP.

## *Chapter 2:*
## *The Company Town*

1
U.S. Department of the Interior, Coal Mines Administration, *A Medical Survey of the Bituminous-Coal Industry* (Washington: Government Printing Office, 1947), xiii. This report is commonly referred to as the "Boone Report," after Joel T. Boone, the physician and naval admiral who supervised the study.

2
Scamehorn, *Pioneer Steelmaker*, 30.

3
William H. Bauer, James L. Ozment, and John H. Willard, *Colorado Post Offices, 1859-1989: A Comprehensive Listing of*

Post Offices, Stations, and Branches (Golden: Colorado Railroad Museum, 1990).

4
Ibid.

5
Scamehorn, *Pioneer Steelmaker*, 149.

6
Bauer et al., *Colorado Post Offices*; Scamehorn, *Pioneer Steelmaker*, 155.

7
Shifflett, *Coal Towns*, 48.

8
Ibid., 52.

9
Colorado Fuel and Iron Company, *Annual Report of the Sociological Department . . ., 1901–1902* (Denver: Colorado Fuel and Iron Company, 1902).

10
Annual Report of the Sociological Department . . ., 1901–1902.

11
Scamehorn, *Pioneer Steelmaker*, 85.

12
Ibid., 149.

13
Shifflett, *Coal Towns*, 66.

14
West, *Report on the Colorado Strike*, 6–7.

15
House Committee, *Conditions in the Coal Mines*, 406.

16
Price V. Fishback, "Did Coal Miners 'Owe Their Souls to the Company Store'? Theory and Evidence from the Early 1900s," *Journal of Economic History* 46 (December 1986), 1012.

17
Ibid.

18
West, *Report on the Colorado Strike*, 68.

19
House Committee, *Conditions in the Coal Mines*, 403–4. While it was true that competition cut into the operators' market in the open camps, they could still operate at a profit as a whole throughout the region. Both Osgood and Jesse Welborn, president of CF&I, testified that their store subsidiaries earned at least 20 percent on their capital investments—a profit margin any businessman would covet. West, *Report on the Colorado Strike*, 68.

20
Steve Surisky, interview (transcript), UCCP.

21
Beatrice Nogare, interview (transcript), HCEDP.

22
Frank Gutierrez, interview (transcript), HCEDP.

23
U.S. Women's Bureau, *Home Environment*, 27.

24
U.S. Coal Mines Administration, *Medical Survey*, 63.

25
*Denver Times*, December 15, 1901.

26
Scamehorn, *Pioneer Steelmaker*, 155; Scamehorn, *Mill and Mine: The CF&I in the Twentieth Century* (Lincoln: University of Nebraska Press, 1992), 84.

27
James B. Allen, *The Company Town in the American West* (Norman: University of Oklahoma Press, 1966), 79.

28
House Committee, *Conditions in the Coal Mines*, 491–92; Scamehorn, *Pioneer Steelmaker*, 55.

29
*Annual Report of the Sociological Department...*, 1901–1902.

30
*Denver Times*, December 15, 1901.

31
Scamehorn, *Mill and Mine*, 87.

32
U.S. Coal Mines Administration, *Medical Survey*, 30, 33.

33
Bob Tapia, interview (transcript), UCCP.

34
U.S. Coal Mines Administration, *Medical Survey*, 41.

35
*Camp and Plant*, July 11, 1903, 20; September 12, 1903, 211.

36
U.S. Women's Bureau, *Home Environment*, 6; U.S. Coal Mines Administration, *Medical Survey*, 45.

37
U.S. Women's Bureau, *Home Environment*, 23.

38
Frank Harenburg, interview (transcript), UCCP.

39
*Camp and Plant*, October 17, 1903.

40
Ibid.

41
*Camp and Plant*, 11 January 1901.

## Chapter 3: The Community

1
Shifflett, *Coal Towns*, 110.

2
John Valdez, interview (transcript), UCCP.

3
John and Caroline Tomsic, interview (transcript), UCCP.

4
House Committee, *Conditions in the Coal Mines*, 406.

5
Ibid., 486–87.

6
McClurg, "Labor Organization," 41; Sarah Deutsch, *No Separate Refuge: Culture, Class, and Gender on an Anglo-Hispanic Frontier in the American Southwest, 1880–1940* (New York: Oxford University Press, 1987), 88.

7
The statistical data discussed in this paragraph and in the figures were derived from the following sources. For 1880: U.S. Department of the Interior, Census Office, *Statistics of the Population of the United States at the Tenth Census (June 1, 1880)...*(Washington: Government Printing Office, 1883), 51–52, 499. For 1890: U.S. Department of the Interior, Census Office, *Report on Population of the United States at the Eleventh Census: 1890, Part 1* (Washington: Government Printing Office, 1895), 12, 613–14. For 1900: U.S. Census Office, *Twelfth Census of the United States, Taken in the Year 1900*, vol. 1, *Population, Part 1* (Washington: Government Printing Office, 1901), 12, 740. For 1910: U.S. Department of Commerce, Bureau of the Census, *Thirteenth Census of the United States, Taken in the Year 1910*, vol. 2, *Population, 1910: Reports by States...*(Washington: Government Printing Office, 1913), 200, 202, 220, 222. For 1920: U.S. Department of Commerce, Bureau of the Census, *F-ourteenth Census of the United States Taken in...1920*, vol. 1, *Population, 1920: Number and Distribution of Inhabitants* (Washington: Government Printing Office, 1921), 96; and vol. 3, *Population, 1920: Composition and Characteristics of the Population by States*, 149.

8
Scamehorn, *Pioneer Steelmaker,* 149–152;
Scamehorn, *Mill and Mine,* 86–87.

9
Scamehorn, *Mill and Mine,* 86–87; Dan
Desantis, interview (transcript), UCCP.

10
Long, *Where the Sun Never Shines,* 277.

11
Scamehorn, *Mill and Mine,* 87.

12
Martha Todd, interview (transcript),
HCEDP.

13
Gerardo Tovar and John and Caroline
Tomsic, interviews (transcripts), UCCP.

14
Ann and Walt Laney and Jake and Cora
Hribar, interview (transcript), HCEDP.

15
Ed Tomsic, interview (transcript), HCEDP.

16
Maria Batuello, interview (transcript),
HCEDP.

17
Al Berte, interview (transcript), HCEDP.

18
Angela Tonso, interview (transcript),
UCCP.

19
Emilio and Gertrude Ferraro and Nick
Halamandris, interviews (transcripts),
UCCP; Al Berte, and Ann and Walt Laney
and Jake and Cora Hribar, interviews (tran-
scripts), HCEDP.

20
Joe Crump, interview (transcript), HCEDP.

21
House Committee, *Conditions in the Coal
Mines,* 402.

22
Frank Harenburg, Bill Massarotti, and

Frank Wojtylka, interviews (transcripts),
UCCP.

23
Long, *Where the Sun Never Shines,* 215;
McClurg, "Labor Organization," 100–101;
Emilio and Gertrude Ferraro, interview
(transcript), UCCP.

24
Deutsch, *No Separate Refuge,* 88–94.

25
Ibid., 104.

26
Louis Guigli, interview (transcript),
HCEDP.

27
Clarence Cordova, interview (transcript),
HCEDP.

28
Deutsch, *No Separate Refuge,* 90.

29
"Mexican-Americans in Colorado" (clip-
pings file), Denver Public Library, Western
History Department.

30
Angela Tonso, interview (transcript),
UCCP.

31
Ann and Walt Laney and Cora and Jake
Hribar, interview (transcript), HCEDP.

32
Louis Guigli, interview (transcript),
HCEDP.

33
Gerardo Tovar, interview (transcript),
UCCP.

34
Alfred Owens, interview (transcript),
HCEDP and interview (transcript), UCCP.

35
Dan Desantis, interview (transcript), UCCP.

36
John and Caroline Tomsic, interview (transcript), UCCP.

37
U.S. Coal Mines Administration, *Medical Survey*, 119.

38
Scamehorn, *Pioneer Steelmaker*, 139–142.

39
West, *Report on the Colorado Strike*, 76.

40
Ann and Walt Laney, interview (transcript), HCEDP.

41
Scamehorn, *Pioneer Steelmaker*, 142.

42
Ann and Walt Laney and Jake and Cora Hribar, interview (transcript), HCEDP.

43
August Andreatta, interview (transcript), HCEDP.

44
Ann Laney, Alfred Owens, and Louis Guigli, interviews (transcripts), HCEDP.

45
Louis Guigli, interview (transcript), HCEDP.

46
Ed Tomsic, interview (transcript), HCEDP.

47
*Denver Times*, December 31, 1899.

48
*Camp and Plant*, August 22, 1903, 136.

49
House Committee, *Conditions in the Coal Mines*, 526–27.

50
David Alan Corbin, *Life, Work, and Rebellion in the Coal Fields: The Southern West Virginia Miners, 1880–1922* (Urbana: University of Illinois Press, 1981), 147.

51
Federal Council of the Churches of Christ in America, Department of Research and Education, "Industrial Relations in the Coal Industry of Colorado," *Information Service* 10, no. 11 (New York: Federal Council of the Churches of Christ in America, 1931), 9.

52
Rev. Eugene S. Gaddis, quoted in West, *Report on the Colorado Strike*, 57. Revernd Gaddis was head of CF&I's Sociological Department at the time of the Great Strike.

53
Federal Council of the Churches of Christ in America, "Industrial Relations," 9.

54
Emma Zanetell, interview (transcript), UCCP.

55
*Annual Report of the Sociological Department...*, 1901–1902.

56
Colorado Fuel and Iron Company, *Annual Report of the Sociological Department...*, 1904–1905 (Denver: Colorado Fuel and Iron Company, 1905).

57
*Camp and Plant*, January 11, 1901.

58
Colorado Fuel and Iron Company, *Annual Report of the Sociological Department...*, 1902–1903 (Denver: Colorado Fuel and Iron Company, 1903).

59
*Camp and Plant*, October 17, 1903.

60
Frank Gutierrez, interview (transcript), HCEDP.

61
Martha Todd, interview (transcript), HCEDP; Frank Harenburg, interview (transcript), UCCP.

62
Clarence Cordova, Ann and Walt Laney, and Cora and Jake Hribar, interviews (transcripts), HCEDP.

63
Clarence Cordova, interview (transcript), HCEDP.

64
*Camp and Plant*, July 25, 1903.

65
Clarence Cordova, interview (transcript), HCEDP.

66
Alfred Owens, interview (transcript), HCEDP.

67
Emilio and Gertrude Ferraro, interview (transcript), UCCP.

68
Al Berte, interview (transcript), HCEDP.

69
Alfred Owens, interview (transcript), HCEDP.

70
Shifflett, *Coal Towns*, 148.

71
Al Berte, interview (transcript), HCEDP.

72
Ed Tomsic, interview (transcript), HCEDP.

73
Gertrude Ferraro, interview (transcript), UCCP.

74
Louis Guigli, interview (transcript), HCEDP.

75
Ed Tomsic, interview (transcript), HCEDP.

76
Frank Harenburg, interview (transcript), UCCP.

77
Glen Aultman, interview (transcript), UCCP.

78
Don Mitchell, interview (transcript), HCEDP.

## Chapter 4: A Miner's Life

1
U.S. Coal Mines Administration, *Medical Survey*, supplement, 2.

2
Alfred Owens, interview (transcript), UCCP.

3
Glen Aultman, interview (transcript), UCCP.

4
John Valdez, interview (transcript), UCCP.

5
*The Denver Post*, March 26, 1922, 1.

6
Whiteside, *Regulating Danger*, 43.

7
*Denver Times*, December 12, 1915, 2.

8
U.S. Coal Mines Administration, *Medical Survey*, xvii.

9
Beatrice Nogare, interview (transcript), HCEDP.

10
*Camp and Plant*, January 11, 1902, 61.

11
Whiteside, *Regulating Danger*, 205–6.

12
Ibid., 74–75, 132–33, 162–63.

13
Ibid., 118.

14
House Committee, *Conditions in the Coal Mines*, 1030.

15
Ibid., 495.

16
Don Mitchell, interview (transcript), HCEDP.

17
Angela Tonso, interview (transcript), UCCP.

18
House Committee, *Conditions in the Coal Mines*, 856.

19
Whiteside, *Regulating Danger*, 86–87.

20
John McQuarrie, quoted in West, *Report on the Colorado Strike*, 81.

21
Whiteside, *Regulating Danger*, 85.

22
Ibid., 73.

23
Ibid., 90–91.

24
Opal Furphy, interview (transcript), HCEDP.

25
Whiteside, *Regulating Danger*, 167, 178, 190–91.

26
House Committee, *Conditions in the Coal Mines*, 502.

27
Ibid., 424–25.

28
Corbin, *Life, Work, and Rebellion*, 130.

29
Colorado Fuel and Iron Company, *Annual Report of the Sociological Department . . ., 1903–1904* (Denver: Colorado Fuel and Iron Company, 1904).

30
Scamehorn, *Mill and Mine*, 89; House Committee, *Conditions in the Coal Mines*, 502.

31
House Committee, *Conditions in the Coal Mines*, 424–25.

32
Frank Harenburg, interview (transcript), UCCP.

33
Scamehorn, *Pioneer Steelmaker*, 112, 152–54.

34
Scamehorn, *Mill and Mine*, 89.

35
Irma Menghini, interview (transcript), HCEDP.

36
*Camp and Plant*, October 17, 1903.

37
Frank Wojtylka, interview (transcript), UCCP.

38
Dan Desantis, interview (transcript), UCCP.

39
John and Caroline Tomsic and Emilio and Gertrude Ferraro, interviews (transcripts), UCCP.

40
Alex Bisulco, interview (transcript), UCCP.

41
Albert and Johanna Micek, interview (transcript), HCEDP.

42
Louis Guigli, interview (transcript), HCEDP.

43
Albert and Johanna Micek, interview (transcript), HCEDP.

44
Gerardo Tovar, interview (transcript), UCCP.

45
U.S., House, *Reports of the Industrial Commission*, 394–96.

46
John Valdez, interview (transcript), UCCP.

**47**
U.S. Women's Bureau, *Home Environment*, 1.

**48**
Long, *Where the Sun Never Shines*, 208.

**49**
Al Berte, interview (transcript), HCEDP.

**50**
Ibid.; Dan Desantis, interview (transcript), UCCP.

**51**
House Committee, *Conditions in the Coal Mines*, 853–54, 869.

**52**
John Tompkins, interview (transcript), HCEDP.

**53**
Shifflett, *Coal Towns*, 77.

**54**
Ann and Walt Laney and Cora and Jake Hribar, and Ed Tomsic, interviews (transcripts), HCEDP; Dan Desantis, interview (transcript), UCCP; *Camp and Plant*, October 10, 1903, 353.

**55**
Dan Desantis, interview (transcript), UCCP.

**56**
Irma Menghini, interview (transcript), HCEDP.

**57**
House Committee, *Conditions in the Coal Mines*, 902–4.

**58**
Ibid., 413; Long, *Where the Sun Never Shines*, 226.

**59**
Rodas Mediniza, quoted in House Committee, *Conditions in the Coal Mines*, 904.

**60**
Ibid., 902–4.

## Chapter 5: A Woman's Life

**1**
U.S. Women's Bureau, *Home Environment*, 32–33.

**2**
Josephine Bazanelle, interview (transcript), UCCP.

**3**
U.S. Women's Bureau, *Home Environment*, 8.

**4**
Al Berte, interview (transcript), HCEDP.

**5**
Albert and Johanna Micek, interview (transcript), HCEDP.

**6**
Maria Batuello, interview (transcript), HCEDP.

**7**
Opal Furphy, interview (transcript), HCEDP.

**8**
John and Caroline Tomsic, interview (transcript), UCCP.

**9**
Albert and Johanna Micek, interview (transcript), HCEDP.

**10**
Louis Guigli, interview (transcript), HCEDP.

**11**
Bill Massarotti, interview (transcript), UCCP.

**12**
Clarence Cordova, Martha Todd, and Maria Batuello, interviews (transcripts), HCEDP.

**13**
Ed Tomsic, interview (transcript), HCEDP.

**14**
U.S. Women's Bureau, *Home Environment*, 5.

15
Shifflett, *Coal Towns*, 82–83.

16
U.S. Coal Mines Administration, *Medical Survey*, 41.

17
Josephine Bazanelle, interview (transcript), UCCP.

18
John and Caroline Tomsic, interview (transcript), UCCP.

19
Josephine Bazanelle, interview (transcript), UCCP.

20
Ann and Walt Laney and Jake and Cora Hribar, interviews (transcripts), HCEDP.

21
Frank Gutierrez, interview (transcript), HCEDP.

22
Joe Crump, interview (transcript), HCEDP.

23
Angela Tonso, interview (transcript), UCCP.

24
Angela Tonso, interview (transcript), UCCP.

25
Josephine Bazanelle, interview (transcript), UCCP.

26
Ibid.

27
Shifflett, *Coal Towns*, 111.

28
U.S. Women's Bureau, *Home Environment*, 3–5.

29
Angela Tonso, interview (transcript), UCCP.

30
Josephine Bazanelle, interview (transcript), UCCP.

31
Emma Zanetell, interview (transcript), UCCP.

32
U.S. Women's Bureau, *Home Environment*, 7.

33
Alex Bisulco, interview (transcript), UCCP.

34
U.S. Women's Bureau, *Home Environment*, 6.

35
Corbin, *Life, Work, and Rebellion*, 92.

36
Papanikolas, *Buried Unsung*, 160.

37
Ibid., 161.

38
Emma Zanetell, interview (transcript), UCCP.

39
McClurg, "Labor Organization," 129.

40
Long, *Where the Sun Never Shines*, 227.

41
Ibid., 276.

42
Angela Tonso, interview (transcript), UCCP.

43
Papanikolas, *Buried Unsung*, 164.

44
Ibid.

## Chapter 6: A Child's Life

1
Clarence Cordova, interview (transcript), HCEDP.

2
Scamehorn, *Mill and Mine*, 88.

3
Don Mitchell, interview (transcript), HCEDP.

4
*Annual Report of the Sociological Department...*, *1901–1902.*

5
Ibid.

6
*Camp and Plant*, December 20, 1901; 28 December 1901.

7
Scamehorn *Pioneer Steelmaker*, 151–2.

8
House Committee, *Conditions in the Coal Mines*, 736–37.

9
Allen, *The Company Town*, 63.

10
Clarence Cordova, interview (transcript), HCEDP.

11
Scamehorn, *Pioneer Steelmaker*, 151–52.

12
Ann and Walt Laney and Cora and Jake Hribar, interview (transcript), HCEDP; Scamehorn, *Pioneer Steelmaker*, 151–52.

13
*Camp and Plant*, January 11, 1902.

14
House Committee, *Conditions in the Coal Mines*, 736–37.

15
Colorado Fuel and Iron Company, *Report of the Medical and Sociological Departments . . .*, *1914–1915* (Denver: Colorado Fuel and Iron Company, 1915).

16
Martha Todd, interview (transcript), HCEDP.

17
Louis Guigli, interview (transcript), HCEDP.

18
August Andreatta, interview (transcript), HCEDP.

19
Don Mitchell, interview (transcript), UCCP.

20
Beatrice Nogare, interview (transcript), HCEDP.

21
Alfred Owens, interview (transcript), HCEDP.

22
August Andreatta, interview (transcript), HCEDP.

23
Albert and Johanna Micek, interview (transcript), HCEDP.

24
Martha Todd, interview (transcript), HCEDP.

25
Ibid.

26
Bob Tapia, interview (transcript), UCCP.

27
Frank Wojtylka, interview (transcript), UCCP.

28
Shifflett, *Coal Towns*, 97.

29
Albert and Johanna Micek, interview (transcript), HCEDP.

30
Pete Baione, interview (transcript), HCEDP.

31
Alfred Owens, interview (transcript), UCCP; Don Mitchell, interview (transcript), HCEDP.

32
Irma Menghini, interview (transcript), HCEDP.

33
Alex Bisulco, interview (transcript), UCCP.

34
Ibid.

35
Alfred Owens, interview (transcript), HCEDP.

36
Ann and Walt Laney and Cora and Jake Hribar, interview (transcript), HCEDP.

37
Irma Menghini, interview (transcript), HCEDP.

38
Al Berte, interview (transcript), HCEDP.

39
Ann and Walt Laney and Cora and Jake Hribar, interview (transcript), HCEDP.

40
Alfred Owens, interview (transcript), HCEDP.

41
Albert and Johanna Micek, interview (transcript), HCEDP.

42
*Annual Report of the Sociological Department...*, *1901–1902*.

43
Ibid.

44
Ibid.

45
Ibid.

# INDEX